My Big [illegible] of Questions and Answers

This is a Parragon Book
This edition published in 2002

Parragon
Queen Street House
4 Queen Street
Bath BA1 1HE, UK

Original book produced by
David West Children's Books
This edition by Design Principals, Warminster

British Library Cataloguing-in-Publication Data

A catalogue record for this book is available from the British Library.

Paperback ISBN 0-75258-761-7
Hardback ISBN 0-75258-760-9

Printed in Indonesia

Illustrators
Angela & Andrew Harland, Mike Lacey, Sarah Lees, Gilly Marklew, Dud Moseley, Geoff Pleasance, Sarah Smith, Stephen Sweet, Mike Taylor (SGA) Ian Thompson

Cartoonist Peter Wilks (SGA)

Editor James Pickering

Contents

Questions and Answers about

Earth and Space

IS THERE LIFE ON MARS?
and other questions about space

WHY DOES THE EARTH SHAKE?
and other questions about planet Earth

WHERE DO WAVES COME FROM?
and other questions about oceans

WHY ARE SUNSETS ORANGE?
and other questions about weather

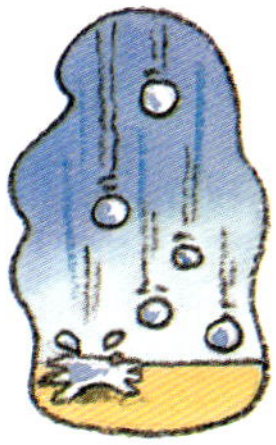

Is there life on Mars?

and other questions about space

How big is the Solar System?

Like just about everything else in space, the Solar System is huge. From one side to the other, it measures a mind-boggling 15,000 billion kilometres!

How many planets are there?

Our planet Earth is one of nine planets which travel around our star, the Sun – the scientific name for this round trip is an orbit. Nearly all of the planets have moons, which orbit them as they orbit the Sun. Other space bodies orbiting the Sun include mini-planets called asteroids. Together with the Sun, this family of planets, moons and other space bodies is called the Solar System.

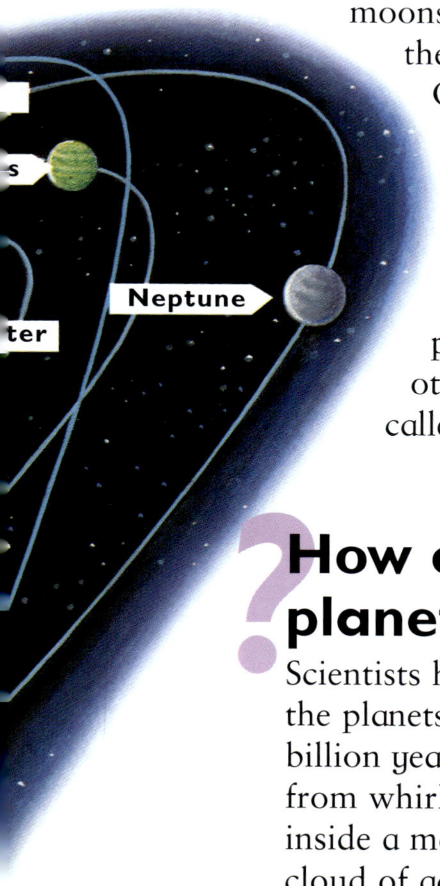

How old are the planets?

Scientists have worked out that the planets were born about 4.6 billion years ago. They formed from whirlpools of gas and dust, inside a massive doughnut-shaped cloud of gas and dust which was spinning around the Sun.

True or False?

All asteroids are tiny.

FALSE. Some are as tiny as sand grains, but others are much bigger than a truck.

Other stars have planets.

TRUE. Scientists have found stars with planets orbiting them. But they can't tell if any of the planets have life on them.

Which is the blue planet?

From space, Earth looks like a beautiful blue ball, with big patches of greeny-brown land and a swirling veil of white cloud. It's mostly blue, though, because nearly three-quarters of our planet's surface is covered in water – the oceans.

Why is the Earth special?

Earth is special because it's the only planet that we know has living things on it. Some of Earth's animals and plants could survive without breathing air, but none could live without water. Earth is the only planet in the Solar System to have plenty of liquid water on its surface – oceans full!

Why doesn't the Moon fly off into space?

The tremendous pulling power of Earth's gravity works like an invisible string, keeping the Moon in its place. Everything in the Universe has gravity. The Sun's is so powerful that it stops Earth and all the other planets from flying away!

True or False?

Earth is just the right distance from the Sun.

TRUE. If Earth was any closer to the Sun's heat, we would frizzle to death. Any farther away, and we would freeze.

There's no water on the Moon.

FALSE. Scientists have found frozen water in rocks near the Moon's poles.

How big is the Sun?

The Sun is enormous! If the Sun were the size of a football, the Earth wouldn't be much bigger than this full stop. The Sun measures almost 1.4 million km across its middle.

What is the Sun made of?

Like all stars, the Sun is a vast glowing ball of fiery-hot gases. The two main gases in stars are called hydrogen and helium – they are the fuel supply for the stars' heat and light.

How hot is the Sun?

Even the coolest part of the Sun, its surface, is 6,000°C – 25 times hotter than the hottest kitchen oven. And the temperature soars to a scorching 15 million°C in the centre! The Sun is enormously bright, too. In fact, it shines so fiercely that even though Earth is millions of kilometres away, its light is strong enough to blind people. That's why you should never ever look at the Sun directly, even when you're wearing sunglasses.

NEVER LOOK AT THE SUN. IT IS VERY HARMFUL TO YOUR EYES.

True or False?

The Sun is running out of fuel.

TRUE. But very, very slowly. Scientists think it will keep on shining steadily for another 5 billion years or so.

The Sun is spotty.

TRUE. Special telescopes show dark patches called sunspots, which are cooler than the rest of the Sun's surface.

Where does the Sun go at night?

The Sun seems to vanish at sunset because the Earth is spinning around like a top as it orbits the Sun. One spin takes a whole day and night, and an orbit takes a year. Night happens when one half of the Earth spins out of the sunlight into darkness.

Earth spins from West to East.

Why does the Moon shine?

Moons and planets aren't as big or as hot as stars, so they can't make light of their own. Our Moon shines because it works rather like a big mirror, reflecting the Sun's light down towards us.

Is there a man in the Moon?

No, although its surface sometimes looks like a big lumpy, bumpy face. The Moon is a dusty, lifeless desert, with no air or liquid water. It's covered in wide flat plains and high mountain ranges, and pitted with big hollows called craters, made by huge space rocks smashing into its surface.

The Moon is about a quarter the size of Earth.

True or False?

The planets don't shine at night.

FALSE. They reflect the Sun's light, too. Venus looks brightest because it's the closest planet to the Earth.

Astronauts have landed on the Moon.

TRUE. American Neil Armstrong was the first, on 20 July, 1969.

Which planet has the biggest moons?

Gigantic Jupiter has the biggest moons. It has 16 moons in all, and three of them – Ganymede, Io and Callisto – are bigger than our Moon.

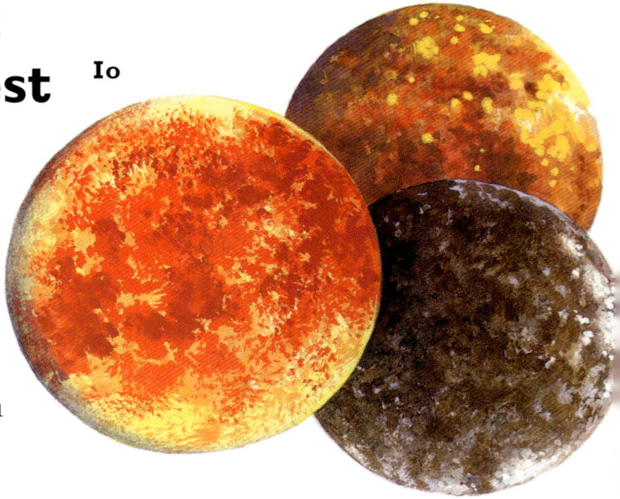

Phobos (left) and Deimos

Are all moons round?

The bigger ones are, but Mars's two tiny moons are potato-shaped. They're called Deimos and Phobos, and it would take you less than a day to walk across each of them. Our Moon is nearly 100 times wider than the pair of them joined together.

What is the difference between a planet and a moon?

A moon is a space body that orbits a planet, while a planet is a space body that orbits a star like the Sun. Moons are smaller than their planet, while planets are smaller than their star!

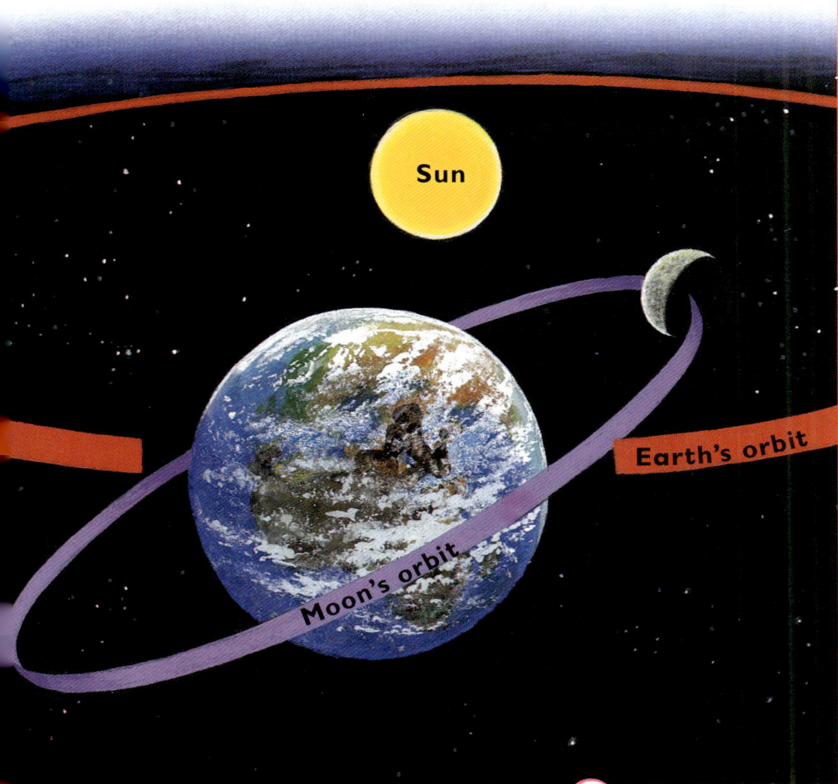

True or False?

Jupiter has the most moons.

FALSE. Uranus has the most, with 20 moons. Saturn has 18, and Neptune has 8 moons.

All the planets have moons.

FALSE. Like Earth, Pluto has just one. But Mercury and Venus don't have any moons at all.

Are there snowballs in space?

Comets are rather like huge, dirty snowballs made of ice and rocky dust. Most of them stay far out towards the edge of the Solar System. Sometimes, however, a comet travels close enough to the Sun for the heat to boil its icy surface into a streaming tail of gas and dust.

Cutaway of a comet

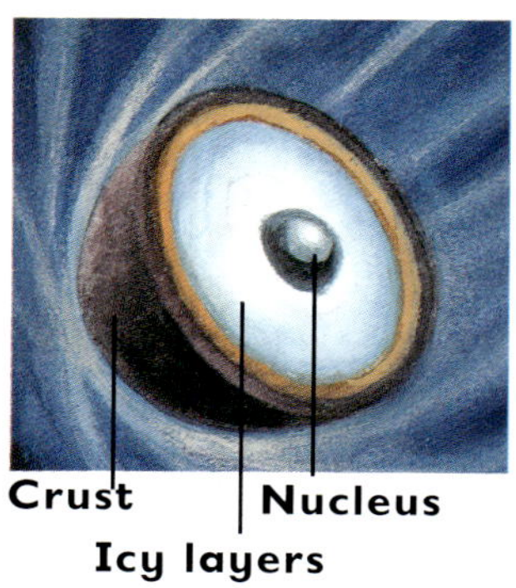

Shooting stars

What are shooting stars?

The proper name for 'shooting stars' is 'meteors', and they aren't stars. Instead, they're pea-sized bits of space rock, burning up into dust as they plunge down through the air around the Earth. They look like fireworks streaking across the night sky.

True or False?

Halley's Comet can be seen from Earth every 76 years or so.

TRUE. You'll be very old when it next visits, though, in 2061.

A group of meteors is called a shower.

TRUE. Some meteor showers can be seen at the same time every year. Watch for the Perseid meteor showers on 12 August.

Which planet orbits the Sun fastest?

The closer a planet is to the Sun, the shorter and speedier its round trip. As the Sun's nearest neighbour, Mercury orbits once every 88 Earth-days – a lot zippier than Earth, whose orbit takes a year. The planet with the longest orbit is Pluto, the farthest from the Sun. Its orbit takes a massive 248 Earth-years!

Mercury

Pluto, the god of the underworld

Mars, the fiery god of war

Uranus was named after an Ancient Greek sky god

Saturn, the god of growth and farming

Neptune, the god of the sea

Venus, the goddess of love

Mercury, the messenger of the gods

Jupiter, the king of the gods

How did the planets get their names?

Most of the planets were named a long time ago, after the gods of the Ancient Romans.

True or False?

Mercury looks like the Earth.

FALSE. It's more like the Moon. Mercury is a dusty desert, with wide plains, steep cliffs, and lots of crater holes.

The Sun looks twice as big from Mercury.

TRUE. But no one has ever set foot on Mercury. The Mariner 10 spacecraft visited and took photos, but it didn't land.

Which is the hottest planet?

If you think the closest planet to the Sun is the hottest, you're wrong! Venus can cook to a searing 500°C – nearly 1.5 times hotter than Mercury, and over 8 times hotter than the hottest place on Earth. Venus is such a scorcher because it's covered with thick clouds of heavy carbon dioxide gas, which work like a blanket holding in the heat. There's hardly any gas at all on Mercury, so there's nothing to stop the Sun's heat escaping.

Venus

Which is the coldest planet?

If you think the farthest planet from the Sun is the chilliest, you're right! Pluto is nearly 40 times as far from the Sun as Earth is, and temperatures there drop to a very icy minus 235°C – more than 2.5 times colder than the coldest place on Earth.

Pluto

True or False?

Venus is covered in volcanoes.

TRUE. They all seem to have stopped erupting, but one of them is over 11 km high – 1.3 times as high as Mt Everest.

Until 1930, no one knew Pluto was out there.

TRUE. It was the last planet to be found. Its moon, Charon, wasn't found until the 1970s.

Mars

Which is the red planet?

Mars is often called the red planet because much of its surface is covered in rusty-red sandy deserts. They aren't hot deserts, though – the temperature on Mars hardly ever rises above freezing point, even in summer.

Will people ever live on Mars?

There are plans to send astronauts there by 2020, to find out whether space bases can be built for scientists to live in and study Mars. So, who knows – maybe one day you will live on Mars yourself!

A space base may be built on Mars.

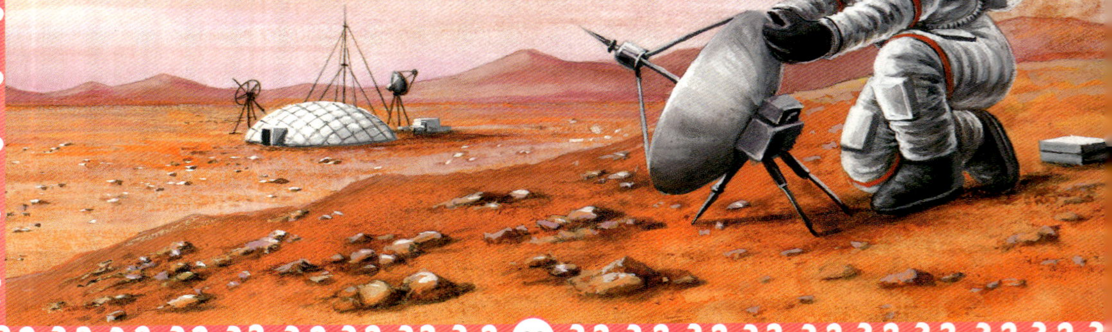

The Sojourner robot visited Mars in 1997.

Is there life on Mars?

Scientists think that if any other planet in our Solar System ever had life on it, it was Mars. They aren't expecting to find green men or other big creatures, though. Instead, they hope to discover fossilised remains of microscopically tiny bacteria. But although spacecraft visited Mars in 1976 and 1997, and sent robots to hunt for fossils, they didn't find any trace of life.

True or False?

Astronauts have set foot on other planets.

FALSE. The farthest any astronauts have travelled is the Moon.

There may be water on Mars.

TRUE. There are ice caps at Mars's north and south poles, which scientists think might contain frozen water.

Which is the biggest planet?

Jupiter is so big that all the other planets in the Solar System could squeeze inside it. Its Great Red Spot is a huge spinning storm that has been raging for 300 years, and it's big enough to swallow up two Earths!

What are the gas giants?

The planets Jupiter, Saturn, Uranus and Neptune are all big, and they're all mainly made of gas, which is why they're called gas giants. Unlike the other, rocky planets, the gas giants haven't got a solid surface. If a spacecraft tried to land on them, it would sink beneath the surface.

Which planets have rings?

All the gas giants have rings, which whirl around their middles rather like hula-hoops. The rings of Jupiter and Neptune are mainly made of space dust, but the rings of Saturn and Uranus are chunkier, with lumps of ice and rock in them.

True or False?

Jupiter is as big as the Sun.

FALSE. Jupiter may be the biggest planet, but the Sun is nearly ten times wider.

Jupiter spins around more quickly than the other planets.

TRUE. Jupiter whirls around so quickly that its day and night lasts less than 10 Earth-hours.

Which planet has the widest rings?

More than 100 Earths would fit across Saturn's seven rings. Some people think that its spectacular, glistening rings make Saturn the most beautiful of the planets.

Saturn's rings

Storms on Neptune

Which is the windiest planet?

Winds howl across Neptune's surface at over 2,000 kph. That's over six times faster than the most powerful hurricanes on Earth!

Which planet is lying on its side?

Brilliant blue Uranus travels around the Sun on its side. Many scientists think that billions of years ago it bashed into another planet, which tipped it over.

Collision with Uranus

True or False?

Saturn is light enough to float in water.

TRUE. If anyone could find a big enough bucket!

Neptune and Uranus look blue because they're made of water.

FALSE. Their blue colour comes from the gas methane. Earth is the only planet with liquid water on its surface.

How many stars are there?

The Sun and all the stars that twinkle in the night sky belong to our huge star group, the Milky Way galaxy. There are about 1,000 billion stars in the Milky Way, and there are lots of other galaxies, too. Scientists think there are 100 billion billion stars in as many as 100 billion galaxies.

Why is our galaxy called the Milky Way?

The Milky Way got its name because we can sometimes see part of it at night, looking like a milky band of starlight stretching across the sky.

Milky Way galaxy

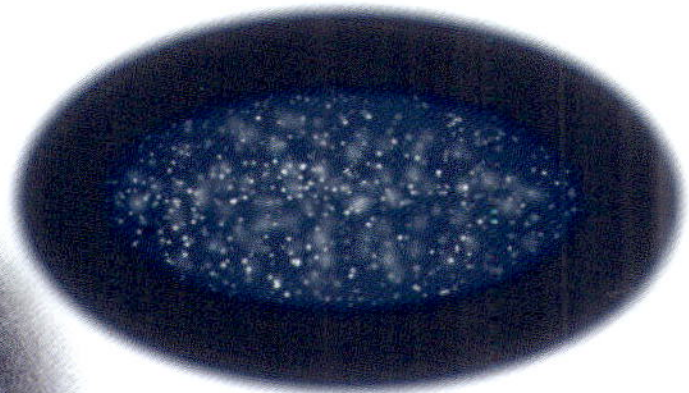

Egg-shaped galaxy

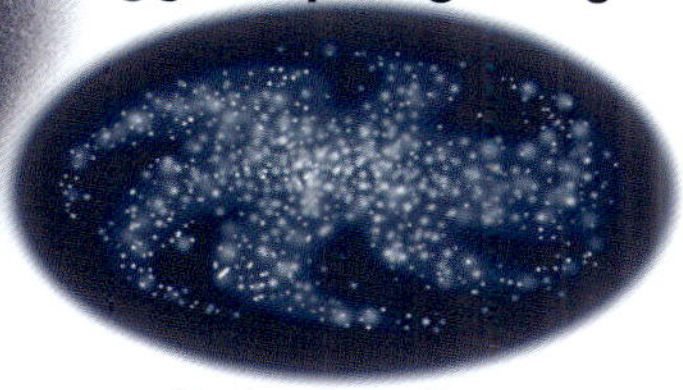

Spiral galaxy

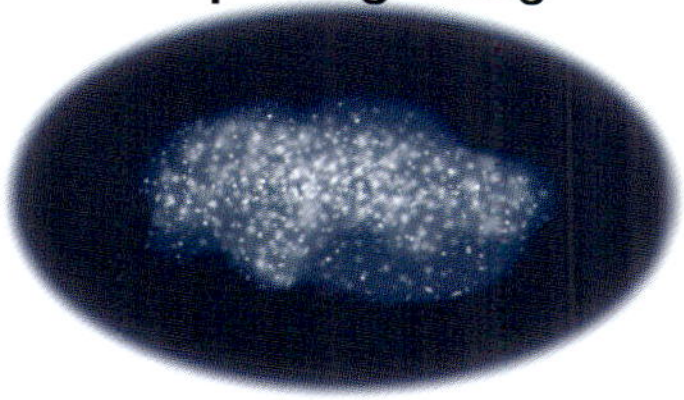

Irregular galaxy

Are all galaxies the same?

No, they come in three main shapes. Some are spirals like the Milky Way – it looks like a whirlpool from above, and like two fried eggs stuck together from the side. Others are egg-shaped or irregular (with no particular shape).

True or False?

The Sun is orbiting the Milky Way.

TRUE. It travels right around the Milky Way about once every 250 million years!

The Great Bear is a galaxy.

FALSE. It's a constellation – a group of stars in our galaxy, which from Earth look as though they form a pattern.

How big is a red giant?

After billions of years, all stars begin to run out of fuel. When this happens to medium-sized stars like our Sun, they swell up and can grow 100 times bigger. These vast stars are called red giants.

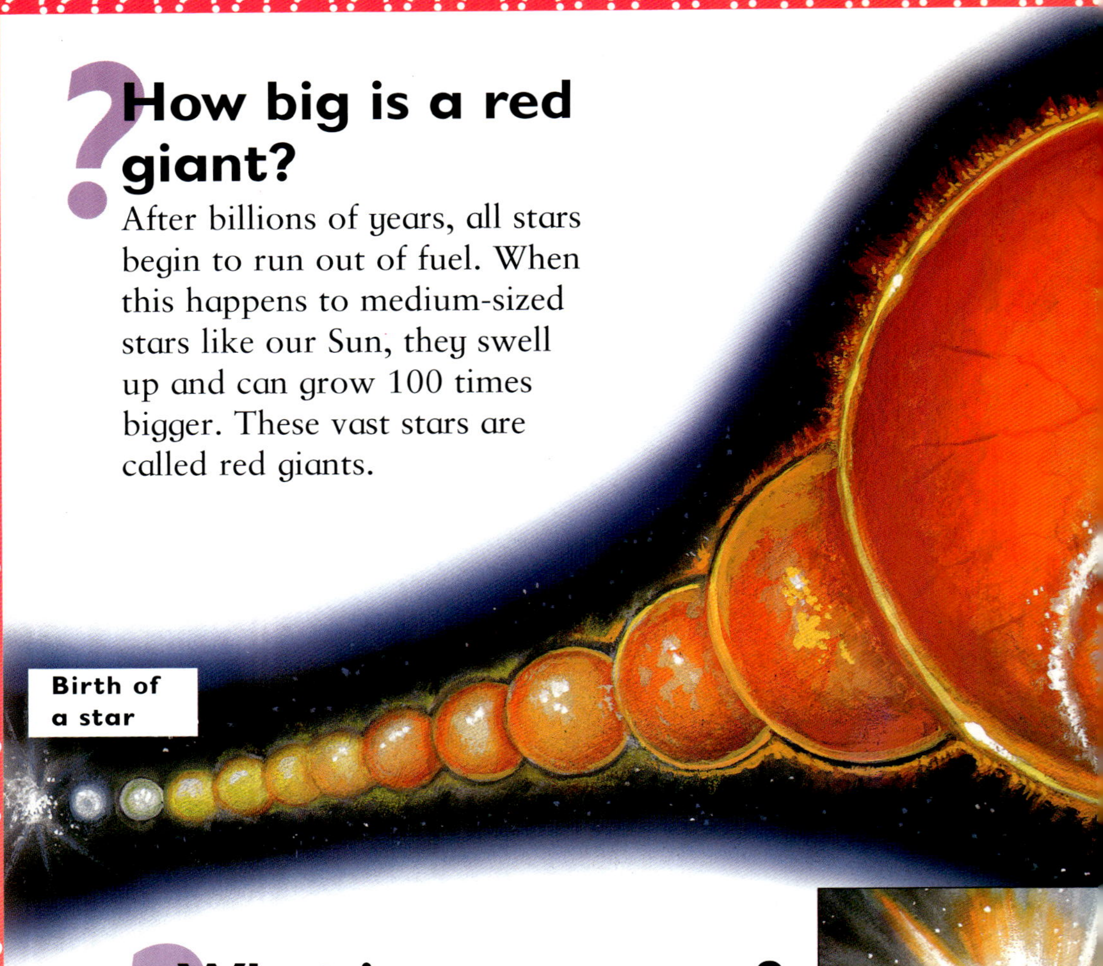

What is a supernova?

Not all stars die quietly. Some are much bigger than our Sun, with a lot more fuel. The more massive the star, the shorter its life and the faster its death. The very biggest stars go out with a bang, in an explosion called a supernova.

Supernova

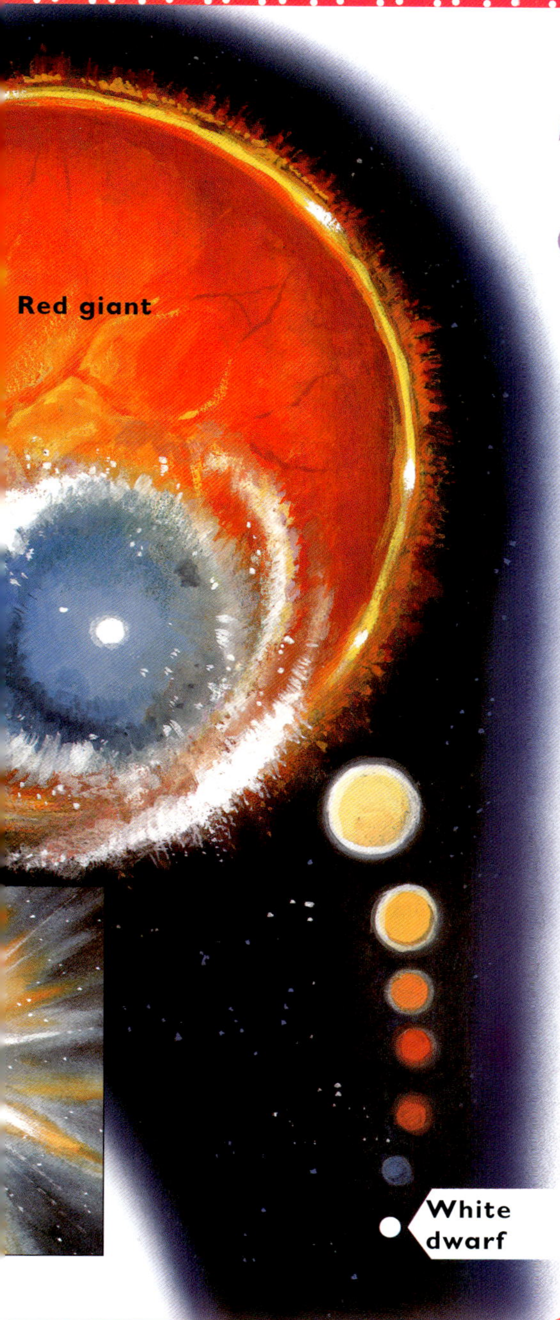

How small is a white dwarf?

After a red giant uses up all its gas fuel, it shrinks to as much as 10,000 times smaller. This is a white dwarf, and although it's small it's still very hot.

True or False?

Some stars are up to 1,000 times bigger than the Sun.

TRUE. These sorts of stars are called supergiants.

A supernova explosion can outshine a whole galaxy.

TRUE. It can be billions of times as bright as the Sun.

When did the Universe begin?

The Universe is everything – you, the Earth and everything on it, the Sun and the Solar System, the Milky Way and all the other galaxies. And scientists think it all began about 15 billion years ago, with a huge explosion they call the Big Bang.

What shape is the Universe?

For many years people thought the Universe was round, like a blown-up balloon. But some scientists now think it might be flattish – like a pancake!

The Universe is still getting bigger.

The Universe may be pancake-shaped.

True or False?

The Universe may end in a Big Crunch.

TRUE. Some scientists think that billions of years in the future, the Universe will collapse inwards and end in a Big Crunch!

The Big Crunch will be the end of everything.

FALSE. If there is a Big Crunch, scientists think it'll be followed by another Big Bang and the birth of a brand new Universe.

Why does the Earth shake?

and other questions about planet Earth

How old is the Earth?

Scientists think the Earth formed about 4.6 billion years ago – a very long time indeed! It was made from a giant cloud of hot gas and dust which shrank and cooled to make a huge ball. The Earth isn't perfectly round, though. It bulges out in the middle and is slightly squashed at the top and bottom.

Earth seen from space

How big is the Earth?

The Earth is enormous! It measures 40,075 km around the equator which is the fattest part of the Earth. It measures about 40,000 km around the Poles. The Earth weighs a whopping 6,000 million million million tonnes.

Where does the air stop?

There is an invisible blanket of air around the Earth. It's called the atmosphere. The air reaches up for about 500 km above your head. This is where the air stops and space begins.

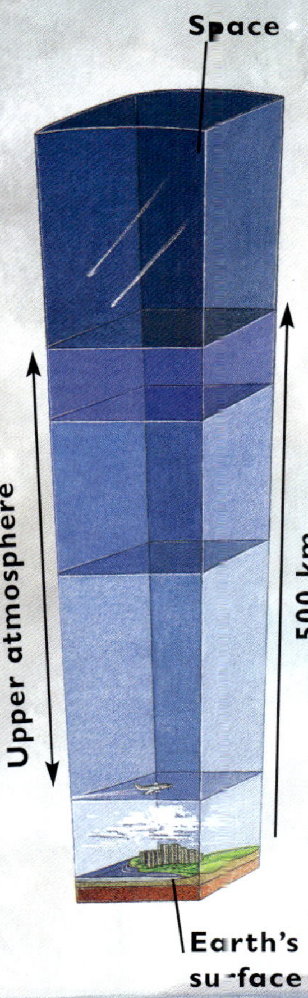

True or False?

The equator's at the middle of the Earth.

TRUE. The equator is an imaginary line that runs around the middle of the Earth, splitting it in half.

Dinosaurs were the first living things on Earth.

FALSE. The first living things were tiny cells. They lived about 3 billion years before the first dinosaurs.

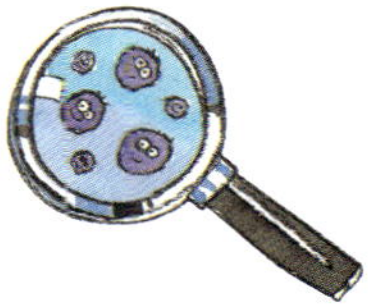

What's under the ground?

The ground is made of hard rock. Underneath are more layers of rock and metal. Some of these layers are so hot they've melted and gone runny.

Is the ground very thick?

Yes, it is! However hard you jump up and down, you won't fall through! The rocky ground is called the Earth's crust. It's about 40 km thick on dry land and about 8 km thick underneath the sea.

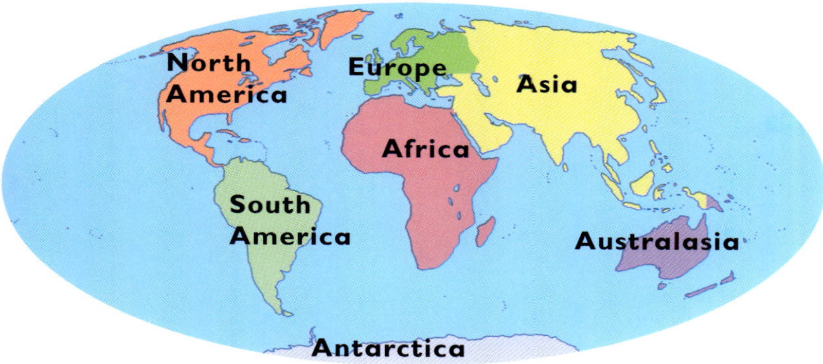

What is a continent?

The Earth's crust is cracked into seven pieces called continents. Starting with the biggest, they are Asia, Africa, North America, South America, Antarctica, Europe and Australasia.

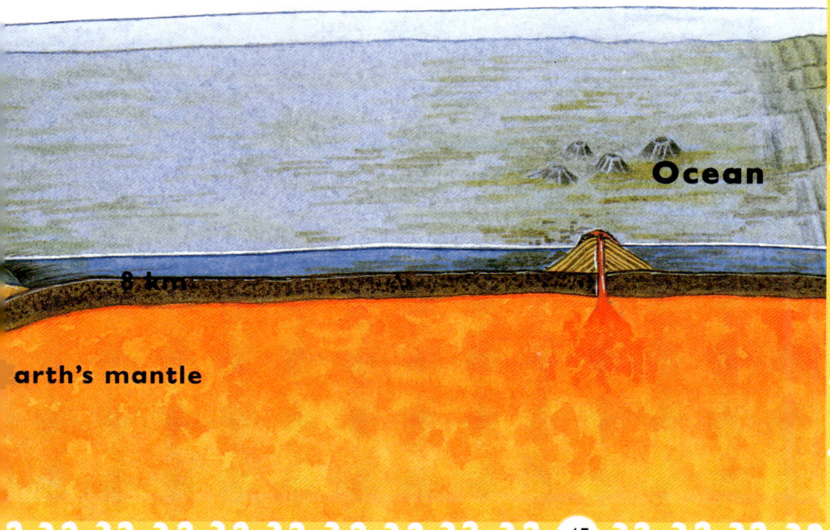

True or False?

The centre of the Earth is icy cold.

FALSE. It's incredibly hot inside the Earth – about 4,500°C. That's about 20 times hotter than the hottest oven.

Antarctica is the smallest continent.

FALSE. Australasia is the smallest continent. It's made of Australia, New Zealand, Papua New Guinea and a number of smaller islands.

How do rocks change?

The Earth's crust is made of different kinds of rock. Each kind is made in a different way. Some rock is pushed underground, where the rock is heated and squeezed. It changes into a different rock called metamorphic rock.

Marble

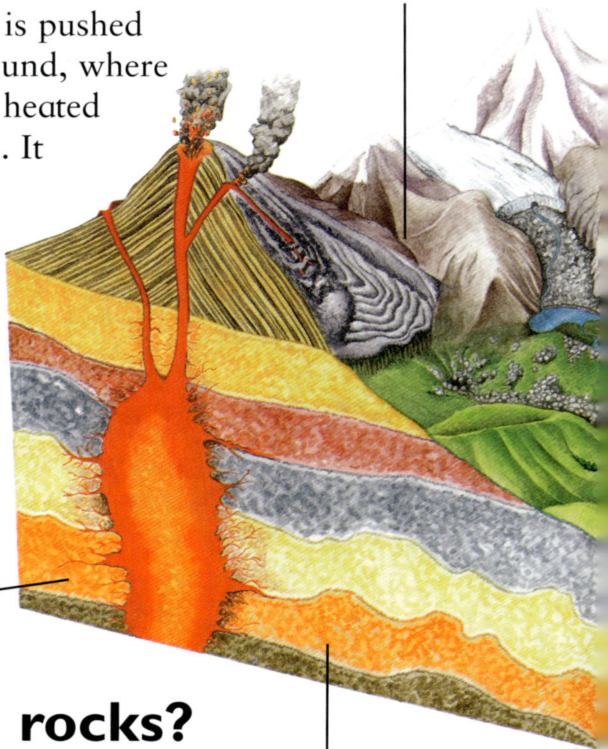

What are fire rocks?

Fire rocks are also called igneous rocks. They are made deep inside the Earth, when hot, melted rocks cool and harden. Igneous rocks shoot out of volcanoes when they erupt.

Pumice

Which rocks are made from shells?

Some rocks are made from tiny grains of rock squashed together in layers. This is called sedimentary rock. It sometimes contains fossil plants and animals. Chalk is a kind of sedimentary rock. It is made from the shells of tiny sea creatures that lived millions of years ago.

Rocks are broken down by wind, rain and ice, and carried away by rivers.

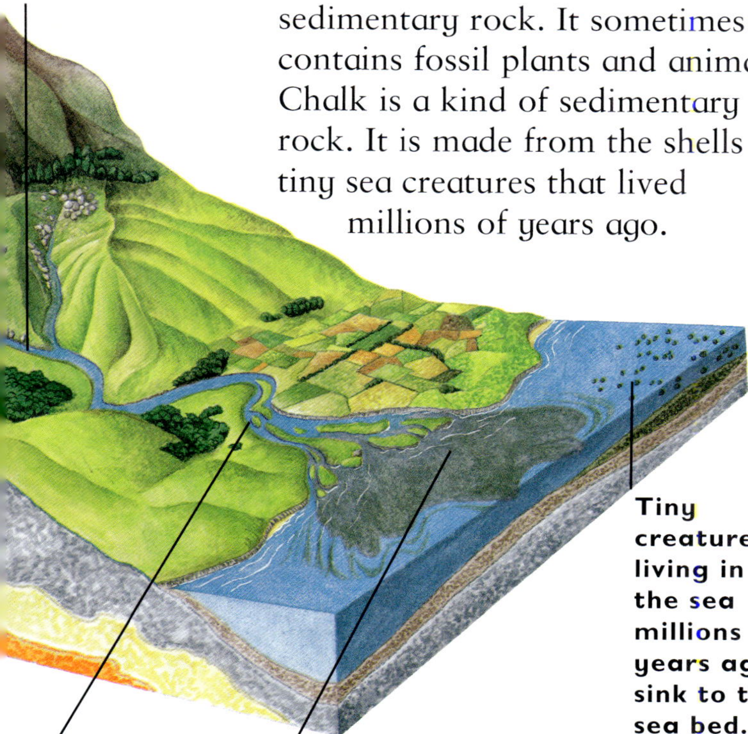

Tiny creatures living in the sea millions of years ago sink to the sea bed.

Rivers carry small particles of rock called sediment to the sea.

Sediment from the river forms layers of new rock called SEDIMENTARY rock.

Chalk

True or False?

The oldest rocks are millions of years old.

TRUE. Scientists think that the oldest rocks on Earth are almost 4 billion years old.

Rocks can't float in water.

FALSE. Pumice is a kind of igneous rock. It is so light it can float in water.

What carves out caves?

When rainwater trickles through a crack in the ground, it eats away at the rocks below. This carves out underground caves and tunnels. Some caves are enormous, big enough to fit a huge cathedral inside.

What's the difference between stalagmites and stalactites?

Stalagmites and stalactites are long and pointed, like rocky icicles. But stalagmites grow up from the floor and stalactites grow down from the ceiling.

Who explores caves?

People who like to explore caves and tunnels are called potholers. They climb down on ropes or ladders. It's dark, wet and cold underground. The potholers wear warm, waterproof clothes and carry torches so they can see.

Potholers exploring an underground cave

True or False?

People used to live in caves.

TRUE. Long ago, prehistoric people lived in caves. This helped keep them safe from hungry wild animals.

Stalagmites can be taller than people.

TRUE. The world's tallest stalagmite is 32 m high. That's as tall as 18 people.

Fold mountain

Block mountain

How are mountains made?

Some mountains are made when two pieces of the Earth's crust crash into each other. They push the rock in between into giant folds. Other mountains are made when huge blocks of rock are pushed up.

Which is the highest mountain?

The highest mountain in the world is mighty Mt Everest in Asia. It is 8,848 m tall. It is part of a range of towering mountains called the Himalayas.

Peak of Mt Everest

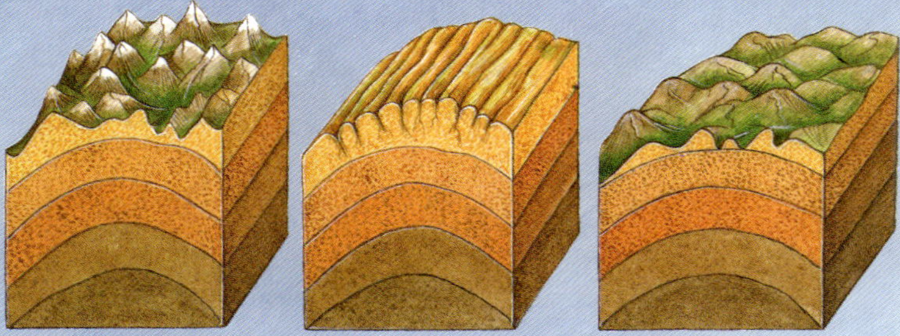

Wind, rain and ice wear down rock.

Top layer cracks.

Mountains continue to wear down.

Do mountains shrink?

Mountains take millions of years to grow. But they're getting smaller every day. The mountains are battered by wind, frost and ice which break off tiny chips of rock and carry them away. Young mountains have sharp, pointed peaks. Older mountains are smoother and rounder.

True or False?

Mt Everest has never been climbed.

FALSE. The first people to climb Mt Everest were Sherpa Tenzing Norgay and Edmund Hillary in 1953.

Some mountains are volcanoes.

TRUE. Some mountains are made when volcanoes erupt and build up cones of rock and ash.

Why are some mountain tops snowy?

The higher you climb up a mountain, the colder it gets. At the very top of a high mountain, it's freezing cold and the ice and snow never melt. Lower down, it's warmer, and trees and plants can grow. Animals that live high up on mountains have thick, woolly coats to keep them warm. Mountaineers must wear special clothes.

Where do you get rivers of ice?

Glaciers are giant rivers of ice which slide down mountain slopes. They begin high up when snow collects in a dip in the rock. The snow hardens and turns to ice, which slides downhill. Rocks and stones stuck in the ice scrape away at the rocks and carve out deep valleys.

Why does snow suddenly slide?

Sometimes a huge mass of snow suddenly breaks loose and crashes down a mountain. This is called an avalanche. The snow races along faster than an express train and buries any people or houses in its path.

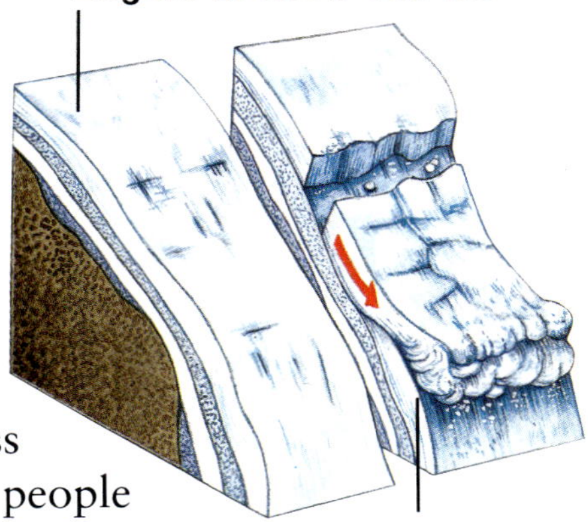

True or False?

Glaciers flow like rivers.

TRUE. Glaciers flow downhill like rivers. But they usually flow slowly, at just a few centimetres each day.

Singing can set off an avalanche.

TRUE. Loud singing really can set off an avalanche. In some mountain villages, singing is banned.

Which mountains spit fire?

Volcanoes are mountains that spit out burning ash, gas and liquid rock. The ash and rock come from deep under the ground. They burst up through cracks in the Earth's crust. Some volcanoes erupt quietly. Others explode with a loud bang.

Why is lava runny?

The hot, runny rock that comes out of a volcano is called lava. It is thick and sticky, like treacle. As it cools in the air, it turns into rock.

Volcanic lava

Do people live near volcanoes?

Many people live near volcanoes even though it's a dangerous thing to do. The ash that shoots out of a volcano makes the soil very rich and perfect for growing crops in.

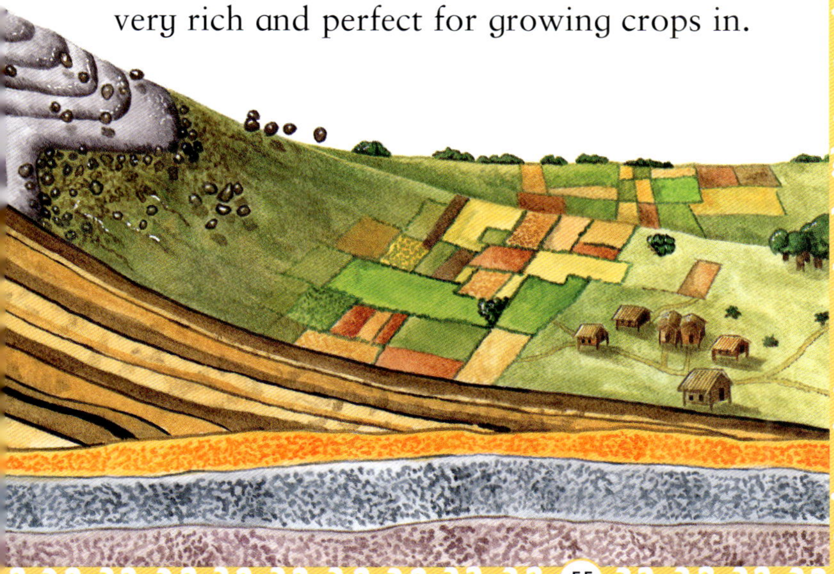

True or False?

An extinct volcano is just sleeping.

FALSE. An extinct volcano doesn't erupt anymore. A sleeping, or dormant, volcano can erupt any time.

The top of a volcano is called a crater.

TRUE. The crater is the dip at the top of a volcano. Sometimes, it fills with rainwater to make a lake.

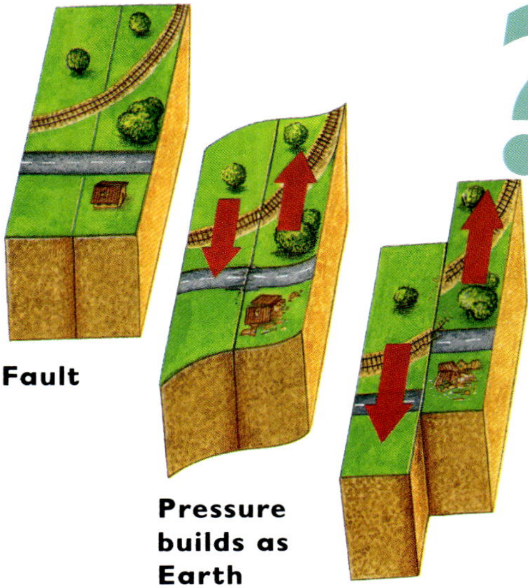

Fault

Pressure builds as Earth moves.

The two parts spring apart.

Why does the Earth shake?

The pieces of rock which make the Earth's crust, drift on the hot, runny rock beneath. Sometimes two pieces push against each other. Suddenly the rocks jerk apart and make the ground shake in an earthquake.

Are earthquakes dangerous?

Big earthquakes are very dangerous. Cracks appear in the ground and buildings and bridges topple over. Many people may be injured or killed, or lose their homes.

Where do earthquakes happen?

Many earthquakes happen where two pieces of crust meet. These places are called faults. The city of San Francisco in the USA sits on the San Andreas Fault. It has hundreds of earthquakes a year.

True or False?

Dogs howl before an earthquake.

TRUE. It's also said that rats run away in panic and goldfish even jump out of their bowls!

Earthquakes last for hours.

FALSE. Most earthquakes last for less than a minute. The longest earthquake ever felt lasted for four minutes.

Where do rivers start?

Many rivers begin high up on mountains as tiny streams. Others trickle out of lakes or flow from the ends of glaciers as they start to melt.

What is a spring?

Some rivers start off as springs bubbling up out of the ground. A spring spurts up when rainwater seeps underground, then gushes back up to the surface again.

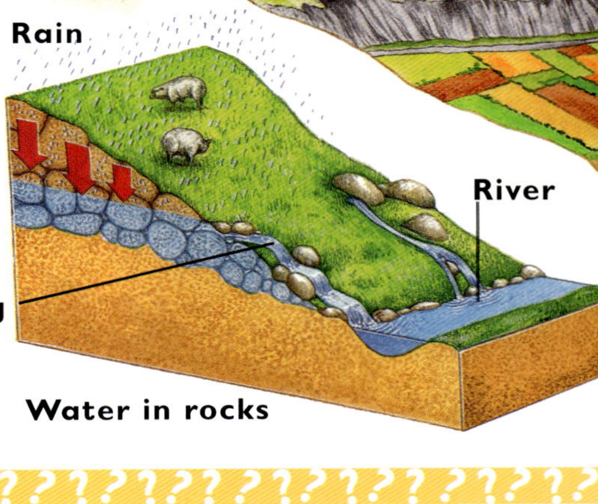

What is a water cycle?

Rivers carry water into the sea. The Sun heats the sea and millions of litres of water evaporate as invisible water vapour. It cools to make clouds, then rain falls from the clouds back into the rivers.

True or False?

Old rivers flow slowly.

TRUE. Old rivers do not flow downhill. They flow slowly over the flatter ground near the sea.

A meander is a big bend in a river.

TRUE. A meander is shaped like a giant horseshoe. Sometimes the river cuts the bend off, leaving a lake.

Angel Falls

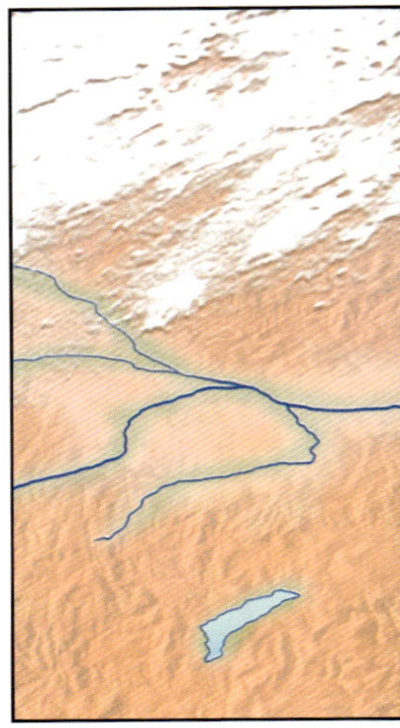

Which is the longest river?

The longest river is the River Nile in Egypt. It flows for 6,695 km. But the biggest river is the River Amazon in South America. It carries 60 times more water than the Nile – about a fifth of all the river water on Earth.

How high are waterfalls?

The world's highest waterfall is Angel Falls in Venezuela, South America. The water splashes 979 m down a tall mountainside. Waterfalls happen when a river flows over a ledge of hard rock. The water eats away at the soft rock below and carves out a steep cliff.

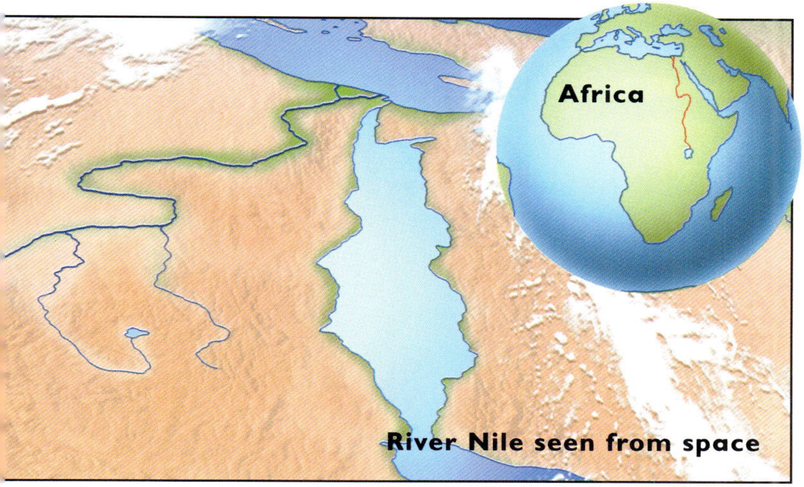

River Nile seen from space

How do rivers carve out valleys?

As a river flows downhill, it carries lots of rough rocks and stones. These scrape away at the riverbed and its sides, carving out deep valleys over many years.

River valley, Grand Canyon USA

True or False?

The D River is the shortest river on Earth.

TRUE. The D River in Oregon, USA, is just 37 m long. The River Nile is about 180,000 times longer!

Some rivers flow underground.

TRUE. Rainwater trickles under the ground and fills up rivers. But not many people have ever seen them.

What makes a lake?

Some lakes form in dips in the ground, scraped out by ice. They fill with rainwater to make a lake. Some lakes are made when a river cuts through a bend. Other lakes form in volcanoes when the crater fills up with water.

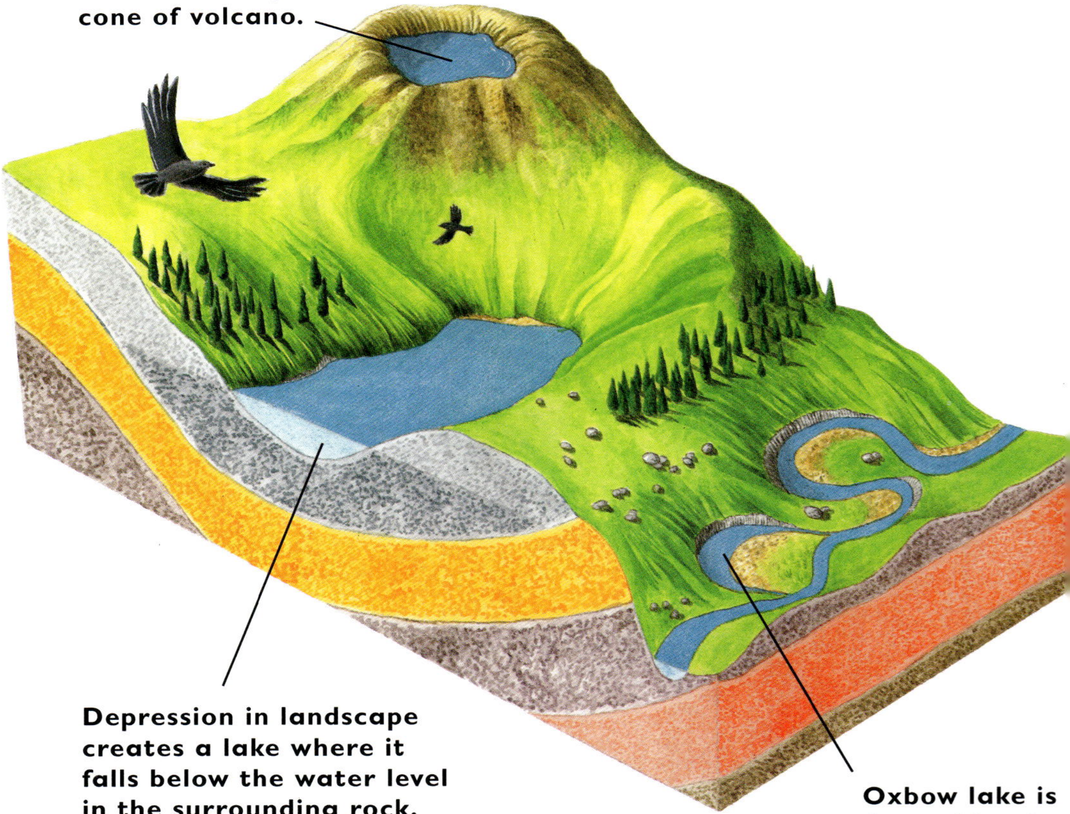

What is a reservoir?

A reservoir is a lake which is used for storing water. The water is used for drinking and making electricity. To make a reservoir, people build a dam to stop the water flowing.

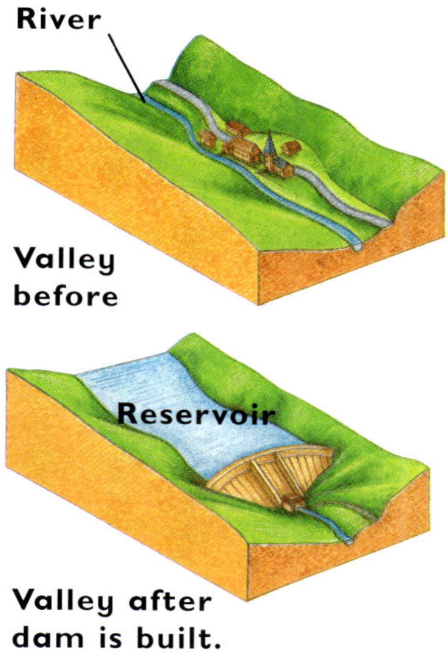

Where is the world's biggest freshwater lake?

The biggest freshwater lake is Lake Superior in North America. It covers 82,100 square kilometres. At 1.6 km deep, Lake Baikal in Siberia is the deepest.

True or False?

Some lakes can be salty.

TRUE. Some lakes, such as the Dead Sea in the Middle East, are so salty that nothing can live in them.

A pond is bigger than a lake.

FALSE. A pond is smaller and shallower than a lake.

Which is the biggest island?

If you count Australia as a continent, the biggest island is Greenland in the icy Arctic Ocean. It covers 2,175,000 square kilometres, nine times the area of Britain.

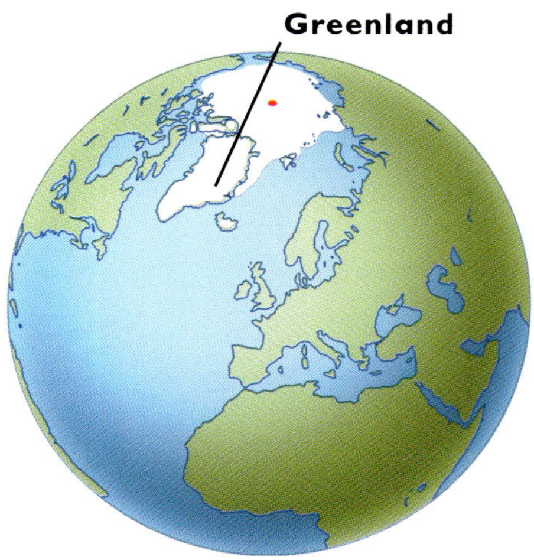

How are islands made?

An island is a chunk of land which has water all around it. Some islands have broken off continents or have been cut off by the sea. Some are the tops of volcanoes which grow under the sea.

Sea level rises to create islands which were originally part of the mainland.

Are new islands ever made?

Yes, they are! In 1963, a new island appeared near Iceland. It was made by a volcano erupting under the sea. The island was named Surtsey, after an ancient god of fire.

True or False?

Some islands are made of coral.

TRUE. Many tiny islands in the Pacific and Indian Oceans are made of ancient coral reefs.

New York City is built on an island.

TRUE. Most of the city of New York in the USA is built on an island called Manhattan.

What is sand made of?

Sand is made of small chips of rock and seashell. The wind and rain break the rocks up. The waves wash the shells on to the beach and smash them into tiny pieces.

Why do some beaches have cliffs?

As waves crash on to the shore, they change the shape of the coastline. The water carves out cliffs, caves and arches in the rocks along the shore. Sometimes, the middle of an arch collapses and leaves a stack of rock behind.

What is the Giant's Causeway?

The Giant's Causeway in Northern Ireland is made of hundreds of rocky blocks and pillars along the coast. The rocks came from an ancient volcano. A story says that giants used the causeway to cross the sea to Scotland.

True or False?

Some cliffs are made of chalk.

TRUE. Some cliffs are made of soft, white chalk. You can sometimes find the fossils of seashells in them.

Beaches can disappear overnight.

TRUE. Rough seas and violent weather can batter beaches, sweeping them into the sea.

Oil rig

Where does oil come from?

Oil is made from tiny prehistoric plants and sea animals. Their bodies sank to the sea bed and were covered by layers of sand and mud. Over millions of years, they turned into oil. People drill holes and pump the oil out.

Why do we mine the Earth?

There are lots of useful things underground, including coal, metals and gemstones. To get them out, people dig deep pits called mines.

Emerald gemstone

Where do gemstones come from?

Gemstones grow in the rocks of the Earth's crust. Some, such as diamonds, sapphires and emeralds, are very rare and precious. They are dug out of the ground, cut and polished. Then they're made into beautiful jewellery.

True or False?

Coal is made from trees.

TRUE. Coal is made from ancient trees and plants which grew in swamps millions of years ago.

Gold is the most precious metal of all.

FALSE. A silvery white metal called platinum is more precious than gold. It's used to make jewellery.

Where do waves come from?

and other questions about oceans

How big is the sea?

The sea is absolutely huge! In fact, sea water covers two thirds of the Earth – that's twice as much as land does. The sea is made up of five oceans. They are the Pacific, the Atlantic, the Indian, the Southern and the Arctic.

Which is the biggest ocean?

The biggest ocean by far is the Pacific Ocean. It covers about a third of the Earth and stretches halfway around the world. All the land on Earth would fit into it, with room to spare. The Pacific is also much deeper than the other oceans.

Key to seas

1 Arabian Sea
2 Baltic Sea
3 Bering Sea
4 Black Sea
5 Caribbean Sea
6 Caspian Sea
7 Coral Sea
8 Mediterranean Sea
9 North Sea
10 Philippine Sea
11 Red Sea
12 Sargasso Sea
13 Tasman Sea

Is an ocean the same as a sea?

Many people use the words ocean and sea to mean exactly the same thing. But scientists who study the oceans say they are different. They say a sea is a particular part of an ocean which has its own name.

True or False?

From space the Earth looks blue.

TRUE. There's so much water on the Earth that it looks blue from outer space.

The Arctic Ocean is very warm.

FALSE. The Arctic Ocean is freezing cold! In fact, for most of the year, it's covered in ice.

Why is the sea salty?

The sea is salty because it has so much salt in it. It's the same sort of salt you sprinkle on your food. Most of the salt comes from the land. The rain washes it out of rocks and carries it to the sea.

Why is the sea blue?

On a sunny day, the sea looks blue. This is because it reflects blue light rays from the Sun. On a cloudy day, the sea looks grey because the clouds hide the Sun.

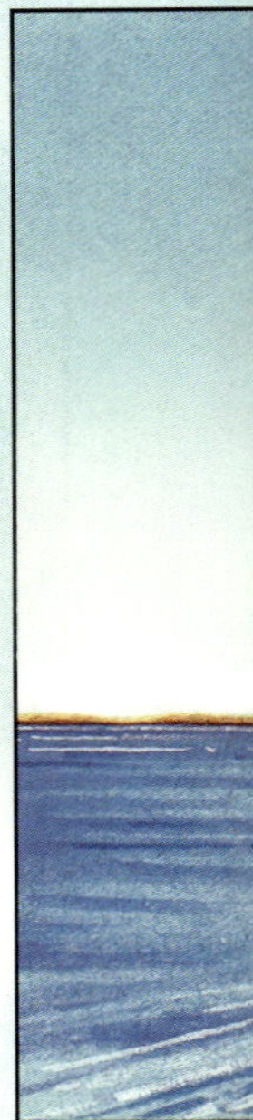

Collecting sea salt

Which sea has red sea water?

In summer the water of the Red Sea looks pinkish-red. Millions of tiny red plants called algae grow in the sea and change the colour of the water. The Red Sea has the saltiest sea water in the world.

True or False?

Sea water is good to drink.

FALSE. Sea water is so salty it tastes horrible. It can make you sick if you drink it.

The Black Sea is very dirty.

FALSE. The Black Sea gets its name because it's full of thick, black mud.

Where do waves come from?

Waves are ripples of water made by the wind blowing across the surface of the sea. On calm days, the waves are small. But on windy days, they grow bigger and bigger until their tops tip over and they crash on to the shore.

Tsunami

Which waves roll as quickly as jet planes?

Tsunamis (soo-nam-ees) are giant waves. They are caused when earthquakes shake the sea bed or a volcano erupts under the sea. They race through the sea as quickly as a jet plane, rear up and drown the land.

Who rides the waves?

Surfers love to ride the waves and the bigger the waves, the better. Some waves in Hawaii are five times taller than the surfers themselves.

True or False?

Waves can break ships in two.

TRUE. In 1968, a group of waves about 30 m high broke a massive oil tanker in two.

The highest wave was as tall as a person.

FALSE. In fact, the highest ever wave was 34 m tall – about as tall as three houses.

What causes the tides?

Twice a day, the sea rolls high up on to the beach, then it flows back out again. The tides are caused by the Moon and Sun pulling the sea into giant bulges on either side of the Earth. It's a bit like water sloshing to and fro in a giant bowl.

What is the splash zone?

The splash zone is part of the beach that is splashed with water as the tide comes in. Animals such as limpets have to cling tightly to the rocks so they're not washed out to sea.

Are there rivers in the sea?

Currents are giant bands of water that flow through the sea like rivers, blown by the wind. Currents can carry hot or cold water. As they flow around the world, they help to heat and cool the Earth. The biggest current is the West Wind Drift around Antarctica. It carries 2,000 times more water than the mighty River Amazon.

True or False?

All seas have a tide.

FALSE. The Mediterranean Sea has hardly any tides at all because it's surrounded by land.

Lugworms eat sand.

TRUE. The wiggly piles of sand you see on a beach are lugworm leftovers.

Is the sea bed flat?

About half of the sea bed is very flat and covered in huge, smooth plains. But the rest isn't flat at all. There are deep valleys, high mountains and volcanoes under the sea, just as there are on land. The only difference is that you can't see them!

What are the cracks in the sea bed called?

They're called trenches, and some are over 10 km deep. Trenches are made when one piece of sea bed crashes into another and is pushed underneath it.

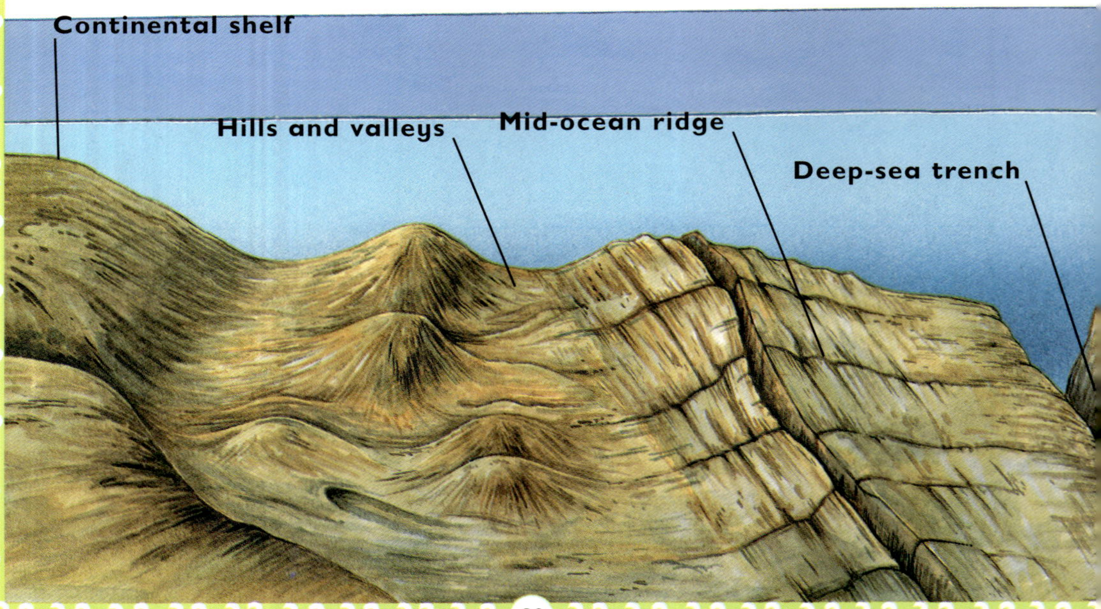

Are there mountains underwater?

There are thousands of mountains under the sea. They're all volcanoes, though they don't all erupt anymore. A long line of mountains stretches all the way down the Atlantic Ocean. It's called the Mid-Atlantic Ridge, and it's the longest chain of mountains in the world. The highest sea mountains are over 10,000 m tall.

True or False?

Some mountains poke out of the water.

TRUE. Some underwater mountains are so tall, their tops stick out of the sea and make islands.

Continents have shelves.

TRUE. Along the coast, the land slopes gently into the sea. This is called the continental shelf.

How deep is the sea?

The deepest part of the sea is the Marianas Trench in the Pacific Ocean. Here the sea plunges to more than 11 km. That's deep enough to swallow Mt Everest, the highest mountain on Earth, with plenty of room to spare.

Who made the deepest dive?

In 1960, two men dived almost to the bottom of the Marianas Trench inside the submersible Trieste. A submersible is like a small submarine. The dive took about 5 hours. Trieste was very strong to stop the men being crushed by the water.

Trieste

What are smokers?

Deep down in the Pacific Ocean, fountains of scalding hot water gush up out of cracks in the sea bed. Chemicals in the hot water colour the water black. Some of the chemicals sink down and build tall chimney stacks around the cracks. These are called smokers because the black water looks like smoke billowing out of a chimney.

True or False?

Divers have walked along the Marianas Trench.

FALSE. If a person dived that deep they would be crushed by the weight of the water.

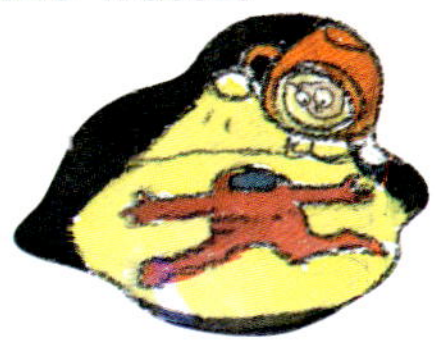

The deeper you go, the warmer the sea gets.

FALSE. The deep sea is as cold as the inside of a fridge.

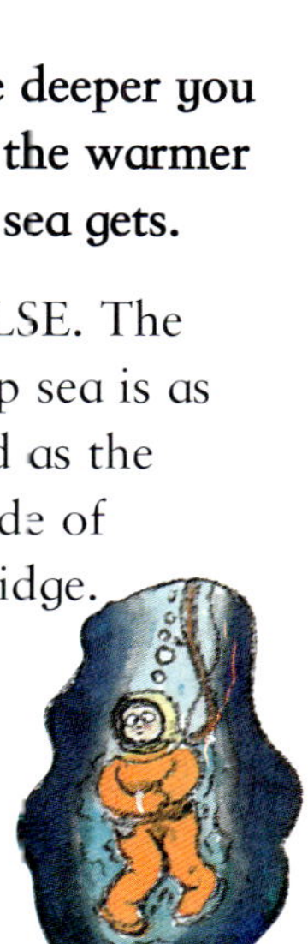

Which fish glow in the dark?

It's inky black in the deep sea, so many deep-sea fish make their own lights. Flashlight fish have lights under each eye. They use their lights to help them find food and can blink the lights on and off.

What has got a big mouth?

Food is hard to find in the deep sea so fish have to make the most of a meal. Gulper eels have very big mouths and stretchy stomachs for swallowing large mouthfuls of food.

ngler
sh

What lives on the bottom of the ocean?

The deep sea is dark and freezing cold. Even so, it's home to thousands of fish and other creatures. Deep-sea fish and squid swim in the water. Starfish, sea urchins, sponges and strange, sausage-like sea cucumbers live on the sea bed.

True or False?

Angler fish use fishing rods.

TRUE. Angler fish use a long fin with a blob of light on the end to fish for their food.

Some fish have legs.

FALSE. Fish don't really have legs but the tripod fish has three extra-long fins for standing on the sea bed.

Coral grows in warm, shallow water around coastlines.

Even when an island sinks below the surface or the sea level rises the coral keeps growing.

How does a coral reef grow?

Coral reefs are made by millions of tiny sea animals. They make hard skeletons around their soft bodies. When they die, the skeletons are left behind, and slowly build up the reef.

Where do you find feathers, daisies and plates?

On a coral reef! They are all types of coral which look like feathers, daisies or dinner plates. Other types of coral look like tiny trees or a deer's antlers. Some even look like brains. Brain corals can grow to more than 2 m across.

Where is the biggest coral reef?

The biggest coral reef in the world grows off the north-east coast of Australia. It stretches for more than 2,000 km and is called the Great Barrier Reef. The reef is incredibly old. It began to grow about 18 million years ago.

True or False?

You can see the Great Barrier Reef from space.

TRUE. The Great Barrier Reef is so big, astronauts can see it from space.

Parrots live in the sea.

FALSE. Real parrots don't live in the sea but parrot fish do. These parrots eat coral.

Where do icebergs come from?

Icebergs are huge chunks of ice that break off the ends of glaciers or ice sheets. They float in the sea until they melt. Only the tip of an iceberg shows above water. The rest is hidden under the sea. This makes them very dangerous to ships.

Is the Arctic too cold for animals?

The Arctic Ocean is icy cold but it is home to many animals. Giant whales live in the sea, and polar bears roam across the ice and hunt seals. Arctic terns and other birds are summer visitors.

Where is the Arctic Ocean?

The Arctic Ocean is in the far north, at the very top of the world. It is the smallest ocean and for most of the year, it's covered in thick ice. The North Pole is in the middle of the Arctic Ocean.

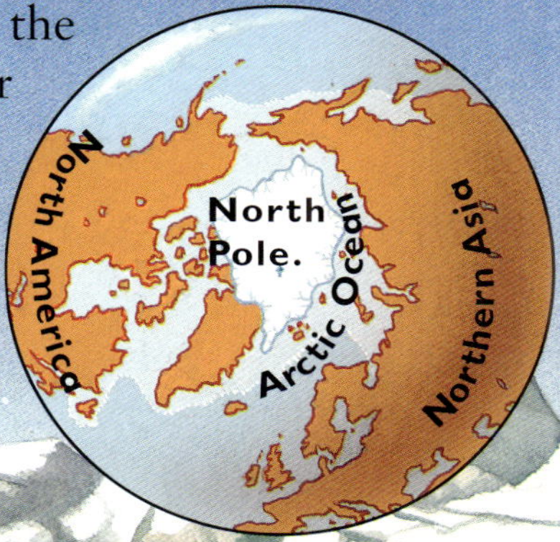

True or False?

Penguins live at the North Pole.

FALSE. Penguins live at the other end of the Earth, around the South Pole.

There's no land under the ice at the South Pole.

FALSE. The South Pole is in Antarctica, where the land is covered by thick ice.

Which animals live in the sea?

You'll find a huge number of animals living in the sea. There are huge sharks, speedy sailfish, seals, squid, turtles, prawns, whales, octopuses, and many more. You can see some of them below. Most animals live in the top part of the sea where the water is warm.

What is plankton?

Billions of tiny plants and animals live near the surface of the sea. They're called plankton. Without plankton, sea creatures would have nothing to eat. Fish eat the plankton, then they're eaten by bigger fish and other animals, such as seals and whales.

True or False?

Whales are the biggest animals.

TRUE. Blue whales are the biggest animals that have ever lived. They can grow to 30 m, and weigh as much as 130 tonnes!

The smallest sea fish can fit on a fingernail.

TRUE. The tiny dwarf goby grows just 9 mm long, small enough to fit on a fingernail.

How do people catch fish?

Some fishermen use simple rods and lines, spears, traps and pots to catch fish. Others use huge nets dragged through the water by boats called trawlers. Some modern fishing boats clean and freeze the fish on board, so they can stay at sea for weeks.

Who collects pearls?

Some people risk their lives diving for pearls, which grow

inside the shells of oysters, mussels and clams. They're very rare and valuable. The biggest pearl ever found was the size of a football.

Who drills into the sea bed?

People drill into the sea bed to find oil. Oil is made from the bodies of tiny prehistoric plants and animals. They sank and were covered by sand and mud. Over millions of years, they turned into oil.

True or False?

There's gold in the sea.

TRUE. There's lots of gold in the sea but it's difficult for people to get it out.

Some fish live on farms.

TRUE. Some fish and shellfish are grown in special underwater cages called fish farms.

Who studies shipwrecks?

Archaeologists are people who find out what life was like long ago by looking at ancient objects and ruins. Some archaeologists study shipwrecks deep beneath the sea. They dive and look for clues, such as coins, clothes and cargo, and precious treasure, such as gold and silver.

Why do they need balloons?

It can be difficult to move some of the objects, especially if they're fragile or heavy. So archaeologists put them in a box and fix it to an air-filled bag which looks like a balloon. The balloon floats to the surface, lifting the box with it.

Can shipwrecks be refloated?

Yes, they can. In 1961, the wreck of the warship Wasa was brought to the surface. It is now in a museum in Stockholm, Sweden. The ship sank in Stockholm harbour in 1628. Two floating cranes helped to lift it out of the sea.

True or False?

Lighthouses warn ships of dangerous rocks.

TRUE. Lighthouses flash a light on and off to warn ships of danger.

Divers have studied the Titanic wreck.

TRUE. In 1985, divers found the wreck of the Titanic in the Atlantic Ocean. They sent cameras down to study it.

Who wears a special suit?

Divers have to wear special diving suits in deep water. Some suits have their own built-in air supply so divers can breathe. One type has metal hands which can hold tools for working underwater. The diver in the picture is fixing an underwater cable.

What is an aqualung?

An aqualung is a small tank of air which a diver wears strapped to his back. A tube leads from the tank to the diver's mouth so he or she can breathe underwater. In the past, divers breathed air through a tube from a ship on the surface. It made moving about very difficult.

What is a submersible?

A submersible is a small craft like a mini submarine. Divers use submersibles for exploring the deep sea and searching for shipwrecks. Submersibles are also used to study life at the bottom of the ocean.

True or False?

Deep-sea divers sound like Mickey Mouse.

TRUE. One of the gases deep-sea divers breathe makes their voices sound high-pitched and very squeaky.

Submarines can dive to the bottom of the sea.

FALSE. Submarines can only dive to about 700 m. The Pacific Ocean is about 11,000 m deep.

What are mermaids?

In olden days, sailors told stories of mermaids on rocks in the sea. The mermaids were women with fishes' tails. Legend said that if a sailor caught a mermaid, she would grant him three wishes in return for setting her free.

What is the Bermuda Triangle?

For centuries, ships and planes have mysteriously vanished in the Bermuda Triangle in the Atlantic Ocean.

Where is the city of Atlantis?

No one really knows. Legend said that Atlantis was an ancient city on an island in the Atlantic Ocean. Its people were very rich and powerful. Then, one day, the island sank and no trace of it has ever been seen.

True or False?

Neptune was the Roman god of the sea.

TRUE. Neptune was god of the sea and controlled the waves and earthquakes.

Sailors thought they would fall off the edge of the world.

TRUE. In olden days, sailors thought the Earth was flat. If you went too far one way, you'd fall off!

Why are sunsets orange?

and other questions about weather

What makes the weather change?

What's the weather like today? Is it sunny or rainy, windy or calm? There are few countries where the weather doesn't change from day to day, or week to week. The weather is blown around the world by powerful winds – which is why a change in the wind often brings a change in the weather!

Why does the wind blow?

Wind is moving air, and air moves when it warms up. This is because warm air is lighter than cold air, so it rises – that's why hot-air balloons float up into the sky. When warm air floats up into the sky, cold winds flow in to take its place.

How does the Sun drive the weather machine?

There would be no weather without the Sun. As it beams down on the Earth, the Sun warms the land and the oceans, and they give off heat which warms the air above them. Some parts of the world get hotter than others, and these differences in temperature create the powerful winds that blow the weather around our planet.

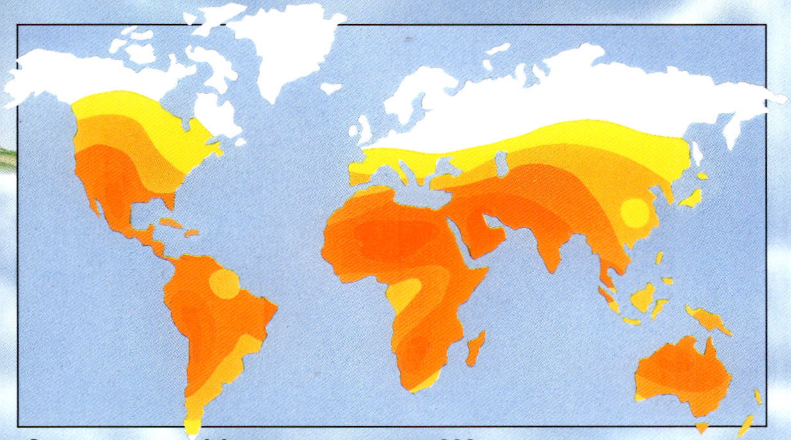

Average world temperatures. Warmest temperatures shown in dark colours, coolest temperatures shown in light colours.

True or False?

There's air in space.

FALSE. There's no air in space. Earth is surrounded by a thin skin of air called the atmosphere.

Airliners fly high above the weather.

TRUE. Weather happens in the part of the atmosphere closest to the Earth. Airliners fly above it, for a smoother ride.

What is the atmosphere?

The atmosphere is the thin skin of air which surrounds and protects our planet Earth. The air is a mixture of invisible gases – the main ones are nitrogen and oxygen.

Where is the ozone layer?

There's only a tiny amount of ozone gas in Earth's atmosphere, but it's very, very important. It forms a thin layer about 30 km above the ground, where it works rather like sunblock, protecting us from the Sun's harmful light rays.

Why is sunlight dangerous?

The Sun's harmful rays are called ultraviolet light, and although we can't see them, they're powerful enough to burn and blister skin. Sunblock creams protect us from the Sun's ultraviolet light, so if you're outdoors during the summertime, make sure you slap on some cream and slip on a hat.

True or False?

There are holes in the ozone layer.

TRUE. The main hole is above the South Pole. It lets harmful rays from the Sun reach the Earth.

You can breathe in space.

FALSE. The air we breathe gets thinner the higher up you go. Space begins about 500 km above the Earth's surface.

How do scientists forecast the weather?

Scientists use special instruments to collect information about the Earth's atmosphere. All the information is fed into powerful supercomputers, which work out what is likely to happen to the weather and produce the kind of weather maps you see on television.

What are weather stations?

These are places where weather instruments record everything from how fast the wind is blowing, and from which direction, to the temperature and the moisture in the air.

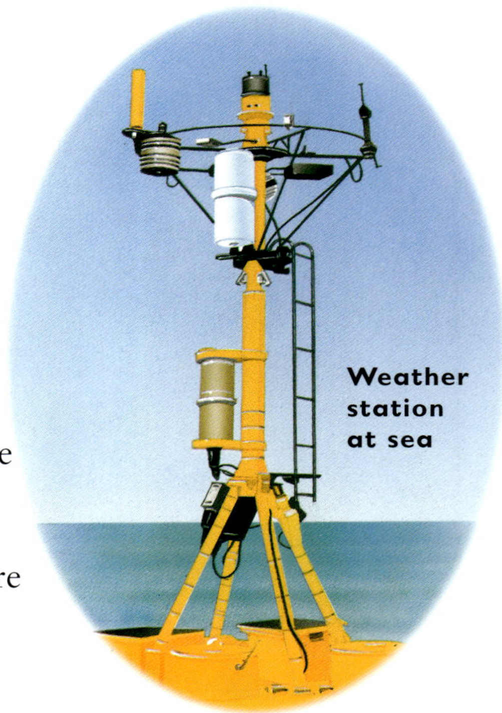

Weather station at sea

Snoopy

Who is Snoopy?

Weather planes also fly high above the Earth. Some kinds are nicknamed Snoopy because they snoop out information with the weather instruments in their long pointy noses. Weather information is also gathered by instruments on ships at sea and satellites out in space.

True or False?

Weather forecasts are always correct.

FALSE. Forecasts for the next 12 to 24 hours are usually correct, but not always! Long-term forecasts are far less likely to be correct.

Pine cones can predict the weather.

TRUE. If you hang one up outside, it will open in dry weather, and close when rain is on the way.

What are clouds made of?

Clouds are made of billions of water droplets or ice crystals, which are so tiny and light that they float in the air. They come from an invisible gas called water vapour, which turns into water droplets when it cools. If the air is really cold, it freezes into ice crystals.

What is fog?

Walking through fog is rather like drifting through a cloud. That's because fog is also made up of tiny water droplets. Unlike clouds, though, fog forms just above the ground.

True or False?

Some clouds look a bit like flying saucers.

TRUE. They're called lenticular clouds, and they form near mountains.

You can't see farther than your hand on a foggy day.

FALSE. To scientists, it's foggy if you can see things as far as 1 km away.

If you can see any farther, scientists say it's misty.

How many different kinds of cloud are there?

Scientists divide clouds into three main groups, with names that describe their shape. Cirrus clouds are wispy and curly, and they're the highest clouds. Stratus clouds form in layers or sheets – some close to the ground, but others, called altostratus, higher up (alto means 'high'). Fluffy, heaped-up clouds are called cumulus.

Cumulus clouds

Can clouds tell us about the weather?

They certainly can. Small fluffy cumulus clouds are a sure sign of fine weather. Get your umbrella out if you see high cirrus or altostratus clouds – there's probably rain on the way. A blanket of stratus clouds usually brings drizzle.

True or False?

A mackerel sky is named after a fish.

TRUE. With its ripples and waves of high cumulus clouds, the sky is patterned like the markings on a mackerel fish.

Earth is the only planet with clouds.

FALSE. Other planets that have clouds include Venus, Jupiter, Uranus and Neptune.

Which are the tallest clouds?

Thunderclouds are huge black stormclouds which can tower 18 km into the sky. That's more than twice as high as Mt Everest!

Scientists call thunderclouds cumulonimbus.

What is lightning?

A flash of lightning is a gigantic spark of electricity which zips from cloud to cloud, or down to the ground, during a thunderstorm. Lightning is so hot that it heats the air until it booms – with a deafening clap of thunder.

Why do we see lightning before we hear thunder?

We see lightning first because light travels much more quickly than sound. You can tell how far away a storm is by counting the seconds between a lightning flash and the thunder. Divide by three to get the number of kilometres.

True or False?

Lightning is hotter than the Sun's surface.

TRUE. Lightning reaches 33,000°C – over five times hotter than the Sun's surface.

Lightning never strikes twice in the same place.

FALSE. New York's Empire State Building was once struck 15 times in 15 minutes!

Why does it rain?

Raindrops form inside clouds, as water droplets bash into each other and cling together, getting bigger and heavier. The water droplets carry on growing until they're too heavy to float in the air, and they fall to the ground as rain.

When do rainbows form?

Rainbows are so magical because they only form when we have sunshine and rain – two things that hardly ever happen in the same place at the same time. The Sun's light may look white, but it's actually made up of all the colours of the rainbow – red, orange, yellow, green, blue, indigo (violet-blue) and violet. Raindrops split sunlight into all its different colours, and we see a beautiful curving rainbow.

True or False?

It can rain fish and frogs.

TRUE. If a tornado passes over water, it can suck them up and dump them in a rainstorm over land.

Raindrops are tear-shaped.

FALSE. They're round, with a slightly flattened bottom.

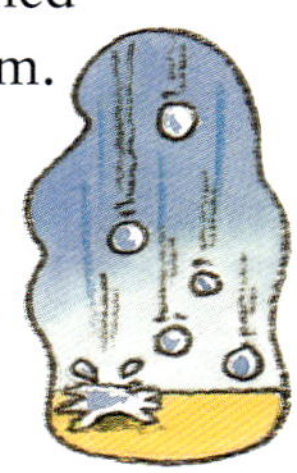

Why is the sky blue?

As sunlight travels towards the Earth, it has to pass through the atmosphere. The atmosphere scatters some of the rainbow colours of sunlight much more than the others. Violet, indigo, blue and green are scattered the most, and they mix together to turn the sky blue.

White light can be made from red, green and blue light.

Why are sunsets orange?

The Sun is low in the sky at sunset or sunrise, and sunlight has to travel farther through the atmosphere to reach us. Yellow, orange and red are scattered the most, mixing into a fiery orange.

What turns the sky grey?

Have you ever mixed all the colours in a paintbox together and ended up with a muddy grey? That's what happens when the sky is cloudy. All the colours of sunlight are scattered and mix together.

True or False?

The sky is blue out in space.

FALSE. There's no atmosphere out there to scatter the colours of light. Astronauts only see black skies.

Red sky at night, shepherd's delight.

TRUE. If the wind is blowing from the west, a red sunset is often followed by a fine day – old sayings like this can make good forecasts.

What are seasons?

In many parts of the world, the climate changes during the year. These changes are called seasons. Winter is the coldest, when many trees lose their leaves. Spring brings new growth, followed by the hottest season, summer. Autumn weather is cooler, then it's winter again.

Winter

Spring

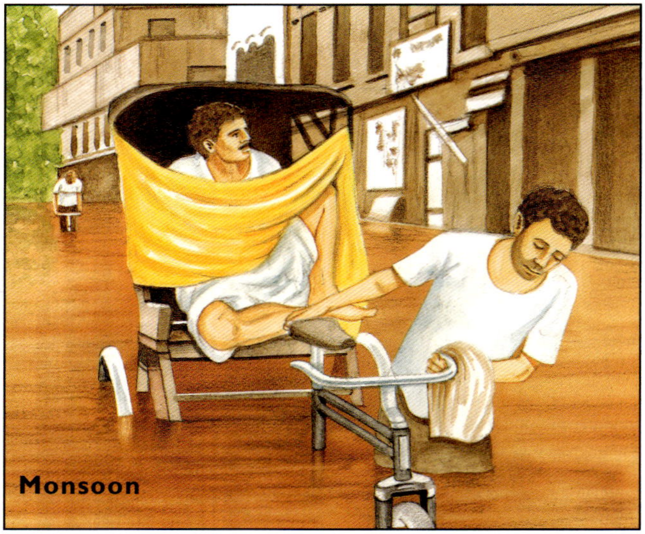

Monsoon

What is a monsoon?

The monsoon is a seasonal wind that brings heavy rain to some tropical countries. In India, the monsoon lasts from June to September, and dumps nearly the whole year's rain.

Where are there only two seasons?

In some tropical lands, there are only two seasons. During the wet season, it can bucket down for months on end. During the dry season, there's so little rain that the ground can bake and crack open.

Dried riverbed

True or False?

January is a winter month all over the world.

FALSE. It's only winter in January if you live north of the equator. In South Africa, it's summertime.

In some places it's dark all winter.

TRUE. Near the Poles, it's dark 24 hours a day in winter. In summer, there's daylight all the time.

How cold is snow?

Snowflakes are made up of lots of tiny ice crystals, which form from water vapour when the temperature inside clouds drops to freezing point – O°C. Like rain, snow falls when snowflakes get too big and heavy to float in the air.

Snowflakes

What is frost?

Sometimes when you open the curtains on a cold winter morning, it looks as though someone has painted the outside of the windows and all the plants outdoors with ice. This is frost, and it's actually frozen dew. Dew forms on clear, windless nights, when water vapour in the air near the ground cools into water. If the weather is cold enough, the dew freezes into frost.

True or False?

All snowflakes look alike.

FALSE. No two snowflakes look the same. They're made up of ice crystals, and each ice crystal is a different six-sided pattern.

Snowflakes can be as big as dinner plates.

TRUE. In 1887, snowflakes measuring 38 cm across fell in a snowstorm in the USA.

What is hail?

Hailstones are lumps of ice which sometimes form inside thunderclouds. They begin as frozen raindrops or snow pellets, which grow bigger and heavier as they're tossed up and down inside the thundercloud. When the hailstones get too big to float in the air, they plummet like bullets to the ground.

Hailstones are made up of layer upon layer of ice, as this cutaway shows.

How fast do blizzards blow?

A blizzard is a blinding snowstorm whose winds blow at over 55 kph. And if that isn't bad enough, blizzard temperatures can drop to as low as minus 12°C – Brrrrr!

True or False?

Hailstones can be as big as bowling balls.

TRUE. Most are pea-sized, but some can be much larger. One that fell in 1970 was as big as a tenpin bowling ball.

Antarctic penguins huddle together during blizzards.

TRUE. Antarctica has some of the world's worst blizzards, and penguins survive by cuddling up in big huddles.

How strong are gale winds?

In 1806, an English admiral called Sir Francis Beaufort worked out a scale of 0 to 12 for measuring the strength of the wind. On this scale, 0 means no wind. By 3, there's a gentle breeze and you can see branches moving. Full gale force is 10 or above – trees are uprooted and buildings are damaged.

Scientists use an instrument called an anemometer to measure wind speed.

Beaufort scale

What is a sandstorm?

During a sandstorm, shrieking winds whip up sand from the ground and hurl it through the air in a scratching, choking cloud. These storms mainly happen in sandy deserts, but they can also happen along beaches or dry riverbeds.

True or False?

Sandstorms can strip the paint off a car.

TRUE. Wind-driven sand is rough enough to strip the paint off any surface – just like sandpaper!

Socks are used to measure wind.

TRUE. Windsocks at airports show wind direction and measure wind speed.

How fast do hurricanes spin?

Hurricanes are terrifying scale 12 storms, whose winds can whirl around faster than 300 kph. They form over warm ocean water, in tropical regions above and below the equator. Most stay out at sea, but if they hit the coast they can sweep away whole towns.

Where is the eye of a hurricane?

The eye is a calm area in the middle of the hurricane, around which the storm winds howl and roar. It usually measures about 30 km across, while a big hurricane can be more than 500 km across.

Hurricane seen from space

Unlike hurricanes, tornadoes form over land.

What's a twister?

Some people call tornadoes 'twisters'. They're another kind of spinning storm, and although they're smaller than hurricanes, they can be even more violent. The heart of a tornado is like a giant vacuum cleaner, which sucks up everything in its path.

True or False?

Gales howl more quickly than hurricanes.

FALSE. Even if they're powerful enough to uproot trees, gales don't blow much faster than 100 kph.

Tornadoes can spin faster than hurricanes.

TRUE. They can whizz around at over 480 kph.

What is clean energy?

Dirty, polluting gases are given off when coal and oil are burnt in power stations to generate electricity. Dirty gases are also given off by cars. But the natural world can give us power without pollution – this is clean energy.

Wind turbines are a clean way of generating electricity. They are powered by the natural energy of the wind.

How can we use the Sun's energy?

Sun power may drive the world's weather, but this uses only a tiny fraction of the Sun's heat and light energy. Solar panels are clever gadgets which capture the Sun's energy and turn it into electricity – without polluting the Earth's precious air and water.

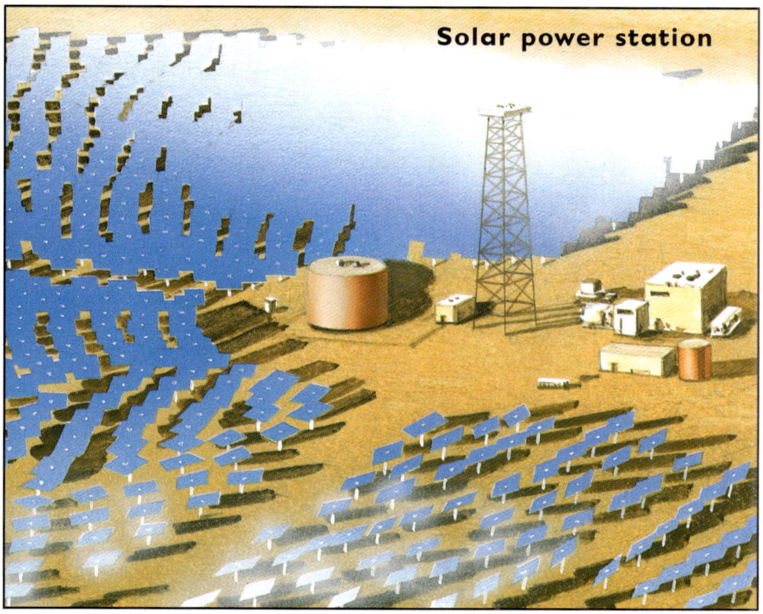

Solar power station

True or False?

We've been using wind power for thousands of years.

TRUE. For everything from drying the washing to pushing sailing boats across the water.

We use far more energy than the Sun can produce.

FALSE. The Sun produces more energy in a single hour than all the people on Earth use in a year.

Questions and Answers about

Science and Nature

WHERE DO SHADOWS COME FROM?
and other questions about simple science

WHAT DO MY LUNGS DO?
and other questions about my body

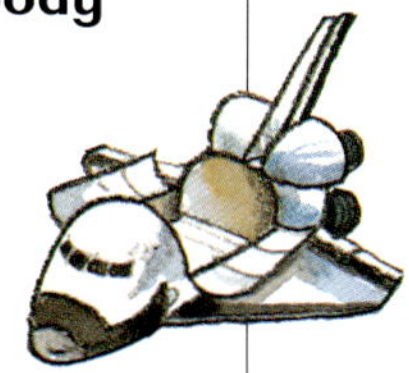

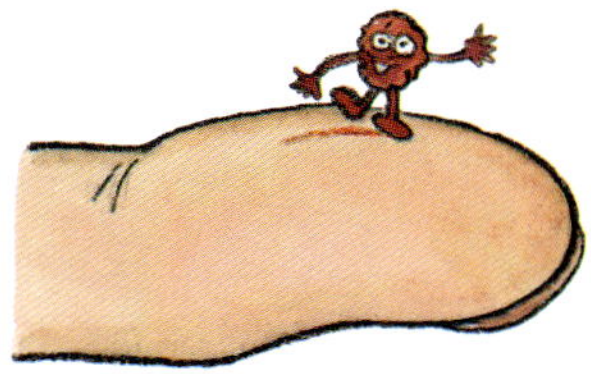

WHICH ANIMALS HAVE SCALY SKIN?
and other questions about types of animals

WHY ARE JUNGLES IN DANGER?
and other questions about things that grow

Where do shadows come from?

and other questions about simple science

What is air made of?

Air is a mixture of invisible gases. The main ones are nitrogen and oxygen, but there's also some carbon dioxide, water vapour and other gases, as well as tiny bits of salt, dust and dirt.

How do we know air is there?

We can't see or taste or smell air, but we can feel and hear it when the wind blows. Wind is moving air – it's what makes trees bend and leaves rustle, and what blows sailing boats across the water.

Is there air in Space?

The skin of air around the Earth is called the atmosphere, and it fades away into nothingness at about 500 km above the ground – that's where Space begins. There's no air in Space, but most of the other planets have their own atmospheres.

True or False?

We need to breathe air to live.

TRUE. Humans and all other animals would die without the gas oxygen.

There's air on Mars.

TRUE. But carbon dioxide is the main gas in Mars's atmosphere, and there's not enough oxygen to keep us alive.

Where does water go when puddles dry out?

Water does a magical trick when it gets very hot – it becomes invisible! When it bakes in the Sun's heat, it changes into the invisible gas water vapour and floats away in the air.

What is steam?

When water vapour hits something cold, it cools and starts to change back from an invisible gas into a liquid. We can see steam because it's made up of masses of tiny droplets of liquid water.

Where does ice come from?

Ice is what happens when water gets very, very cold – it freezes into a solid. Most materials will change from a liquid into a gas if they get hot enough, and from a liquid into a solid if they get cold enough.

True or False?

Your body is mainly water.

TRUE. About 65% of your body is water. Elephants are 70% water and worms are 80%.

Icebergs can be as big as skyscrapers.

TRUE. Believe it or not, the tallest iceberg ever seen was well over 150 m high!

Why do balloons get bigger?

One reason balloons get bigger is because you're blowing lots of air into them. The other is because they're made of a stretchy material called rubber. But don't forget to tie a knot to hold the air in, or your balloons will shrink again very quickly!

Why do balloons float?

Things float upwards when they're lighter than their surroundings. Air-filled balloons are roughly the same weight as the air around them, which is why they don't float all that well. The best floaters are filled with a gas that's much lighter than air. It's called helium, and it's used in airships as well as in party balloons.

True or False?

You cannot weigh air.

FALSE. Like everything on Earth, air has weight – 4,000 balloons would weigh the same as a tub of ice cream.

Most fish use balloons to help them float.

TRUE. Most fish have a gas-filled bag called a swim bladder inside them, which helps them float.

Why do rubber ducks float in the bath?

Air is lighter than water, and one reason a rubber duck floats is because it's stuffed full of air. The water helps, too, because it pushes up on the duck. This upwards push is called upthrust.

Why does the water level rise when I get in the bath?

When you get in the bath, your body pushes the water out of the way. The only place the water can go is up, so the water level rises.

Why does the soap sink?

Things will float in water only if they are lighter than the amount of water they push aside. If they are heavier, the water's upthrust isn't strong enough to hold them up. A bar of soap will sink if it's heavier than the amount of water it pushes aside.

True or False?

It's easier to float in salty water.

TRUE. Salty water has more upthrust than fresh water.

Showers are a modern invention.

FALSE. The first showers were taken as long as 2,500 years ago, by the Ancient Greeks.

Where does sugar go in hot drinks?

Sugar doesn't just vanish in hot drinks, it does the same trick in cold ones. It doesn't completely disappear, though – you can taste it's there. You can't see the sugar, because it spreads completely into the water. We call this dissolving.

Why do fizzy drinks have bubbles?

The bubbles in fizzy drinks are the gas carbon dioxide. You can't see them when the top is on the bottle because the carbon dioxide is dissolved in the water. Lots of carbon dioxide is squashed into the drink, and when you open the bottle, the gas escapes as bubbles.

True or False?

Fish breathe air just as we do.

FALSE. They breathe the oxygen dissolved in water.

Salt comes from sea water.

TRUE. It's dissolved in sea water. To separate it, sea water is heated until the water changes into gas and floats away, leaving the salt behind.

Why can't we see in the dark?

We can't see in the dark because we can't see without light. Objects like trees and houses don't give off their own light, even in the daytime. We can only see them because sunlight is bouncing off them into our eyes. This bouncing off is called reflection.

Why can I see myself in a mirror?

When light hits something rough like a blanket, it scatters in all directions – like spilling sugar. But when light hits something smooth like a mirror, it comes straight back – like a ball bouncing off a wall. You see yourself in a mirror because light bounces off your face towards the mirror, and then straight back into your eyes.

True or False?

The Moon shines with its own light.

FALSE. Moonlight is sunshine bouncing off the Moon towards us.

Cats have mirrors in their eyes.

TRUE. Cats' eyes have a mirror-like layer to help them see in the dark.

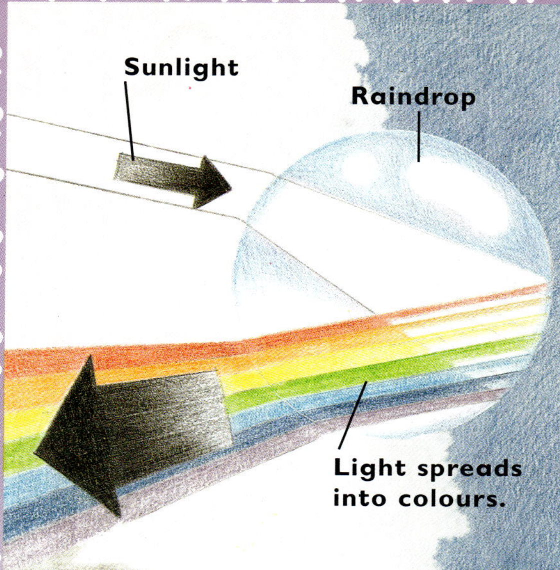

Is light white?

Light may look white sometimes, but it's really a mixture of all the colours of the rainbow – red, orange, yellow, green, blue, indigo (violet-blue), violet.

Why do rainbows happen?

Rainbows happen when sunlight passes through water drops. The water drops make white light spread into all its colours, and we see a rainbow.

Why is grass green?

When light hits something, only some of its colours bounce back. Grass looks green because only green light bounces off it – the other colours of light are swallowed up.

True or False?

You can visit the end of the rainbow.

FALSE. When you move, the rainbow seems to move with you – you always stay in the middle of the rainbow.

Birds can't see colours.

FALSE. Although lots of animals can't see colours, birds can.

Why does opening the curtains make it light?

Light can pass through some materials, such as window glass, but not others. When materials let light through, we call them transparent.

Where do shadows come from?

Your body isn't transparent, so it blocks the light and makes the dark patch we call a shadow form. You can test this out on a sunny day – to see your shadow, stand with your back to the Sun.

Why does drawing the curtains make it dark?

When things don't let light through, we call them opaque. If curtains are made of thick, heavy cloth, they can be opaque enough to block light and make rooms dark, even during the day.

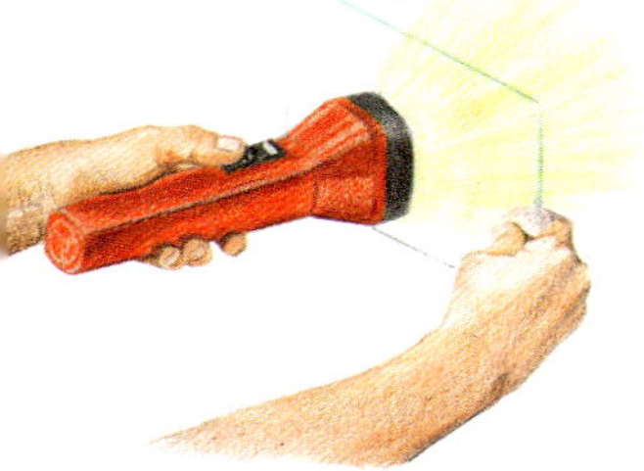

Transparent

Opaque

True or False?

You can jump on your shadow.

FALSE. Your shadow moves with you.

You can tell the time with shadows.

TRUE. Shadow clocks are called sundials.

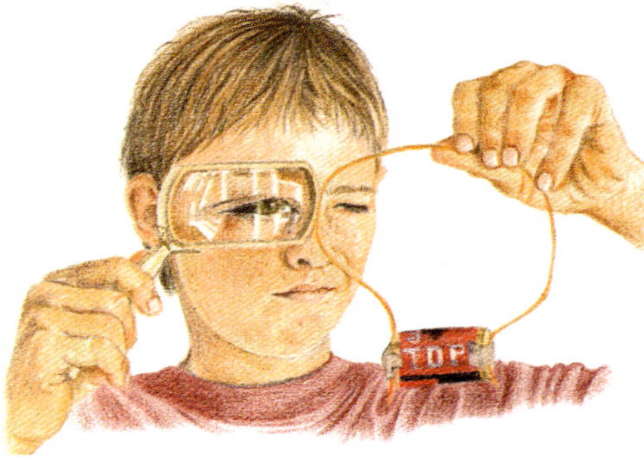

Why can't we see electricity?

Electricity is made of things called electrons, which are so tiny that we can't see them.

Where does electricity come from?

Most of our electricity is made in power stations by machines called generators. Electricity is a kind of energy and it flows into our homes, schools and towns through cables buried beneath our feet or wires hanging high over our heads.

Electricity is very, very dangerous – always ask a grown-up before you use something electrical.

How can I make electricity?

You can make a safe kind of electricity by rubbing a balloon against a nylon jumper. It's called static electricity and it has pulling power – test this out by sticking the balloon on a wall.

True or False?

Wind is used to make electricity.

TRUE. Electricity generators are powered by wind, water, coal, oil, gas or nuclear fuel.

Our electricity comes from the sky.

FALSE. Lightning is a flash of static electricity, but it isn't used to power things.

Why do things stop working when you switch them off?

Electricity only works when it can flow all the way around a loop called a circuit. Turning off a switch breaks the circuit, stopping the flow and turning electrical things like lights off. Turning a switch on joins the circuit and makes them work again.

Ask a grown-up to help you make this simple switch and circuit

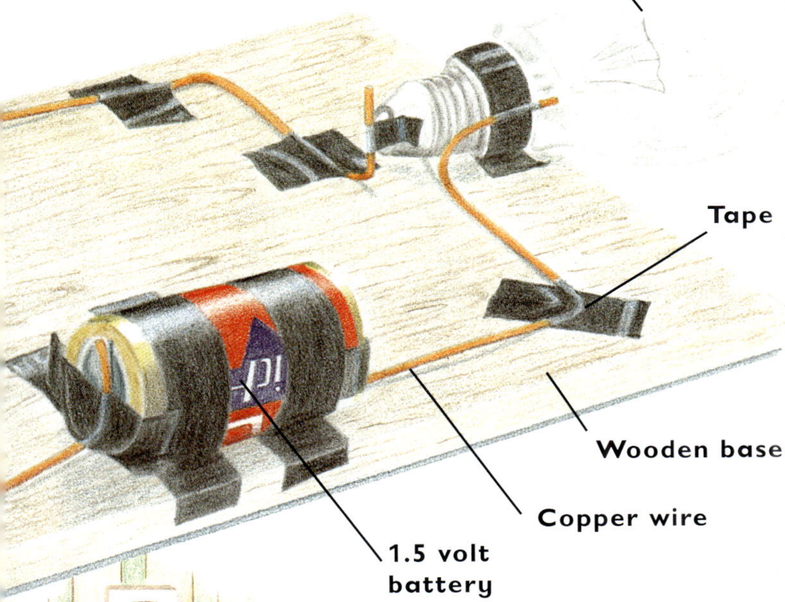

How do batteries make electricity?

There are metals and other special chemicals inside a battery, which can change to make electricity. The chemicals are dangerous, though, so never open a battery to look at them.

True or False?

A lemon can be a battery.

TRUE. If you stick copper wire and a steel paper clip in a lemon, the metals will mix with the lemon juice and make electricity.

Spacecraft have batteries.

TRUE. The batteries make electricity for lights and machines.

How can I see sound?

Sound is a kind of energy which happens when something vibrates, or shakes, and makes the air around it vibrate as well. The vibrations travel through the air into your ears, and you hear sounds. You can see sound energy if you sprinkle sugar on a drum and then hit it with a stick. The vibrations will make the sugar shake up and down.

How do sounds travel along telephone wires?

Telephones have a microphone in them which changes sound energy into electricity. The electricity flows through wires to another telephone, where a small speaker changes the electricity back into sound energy.

True or False?

All phones need wires.

FALSE. Mobile phones change sound energy into radio signals, which can travel a long way without wires.

You can't hear sounds underwater.

FALSE. Sounds can travel through water and all sorts of other materials.

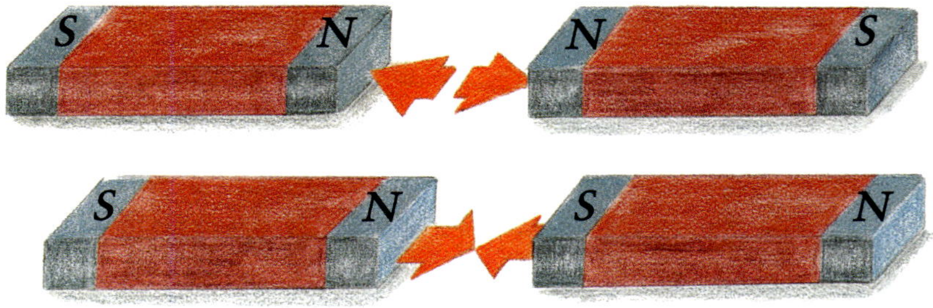

How do magnets push and pull?

The two ends of a magnet are called its north and south poles. If you have two magnets, the north pole of one will attract (pull) the south pole of the other towards it. Two north poles or two south poles will repel (push away) each other.

Do magnets have glue in them?

No, magnets work because they have an invisible force called magnetism. Most magnets are made of iron or steel, and their magnetism pulls objects made of iron or steel towards them.

How do magnets help explorers?

Magnets are used in compasses because if a magnet can move freely, its north pole will always swing round to point towards the Earth's North Pole. You can test this out by hanging a bar magnet on a piece of string.

Magnet lines up with north

True or False?

The Earth is a magnet.

TRUE. Its south magnetic pole is near the North Pole, and its north magnetic pole is near the South Pole.

Your fingers will stick to a magnet.

FALSE. Only iron or steel objects will stick to a magnet.

Why are slides slippery?

Friction is a slowing force which happens when two surfaces rub against each other. Rough surfaces create stronger friction than smooth ones do, which is why slides are given smooth slippery surfaces. Can you imagine how difficult it would be to slide down a rough concrete ramp?

Why do bikes have brakes?

Brakes help a bike to stop, of course – but do you know why? It's because brakes use friction. When you squeeze the brakes, rubber blocks press against the wheels. The friction between the blocks and the wheels slows your bike down.

True or False?

Friction helps you walk.

TRUE. Friction between your shoes and the ground helps you to grip and move forward.

The first bikes didn't have brakes.

TRUE. When the earliest bicycles were made in the 1790s, they didn't have brakes or pedals.

Why do I fall over?

You might start to fall because you trip, but it's the invisible force of gravity that makes you end up on the ground. Gravity is a real downer – it's what tugs everything on Earth towards the ground and stops things like footballs from flying off into Space.

How fast do skydivers fall?

When skydivers jump out of an aeroplane they drop towards the ground at about 190 kph. Opening a parachute slows the skydiver down to about 20 kph – but that's still a lot faster than you can run!

What makes things heavy?

Gravity does! Weight is the effect of gravity on an object's mass – the amount of stuff it's made of. The more mass something has, the more gravity tugs it down and the heavier it is.

True or False?

The Moon has no gravity.

FALSE. Like everything in the Universe, the Moon has gravity. It's about one-sixth of the Earth's.

Elephants are the heaviest animals.

FALSE. Blue whales can weigh 140 tonnes, which is heavier than 25 elephants.

What do my lungs do?

and other questions about my body

Am I special?

Yes, because there's only one person like you in the whole wide world! We all have different coloured hair, skin and eyes, we may be tall or short and we all walk and talk differently.

What do you look like?

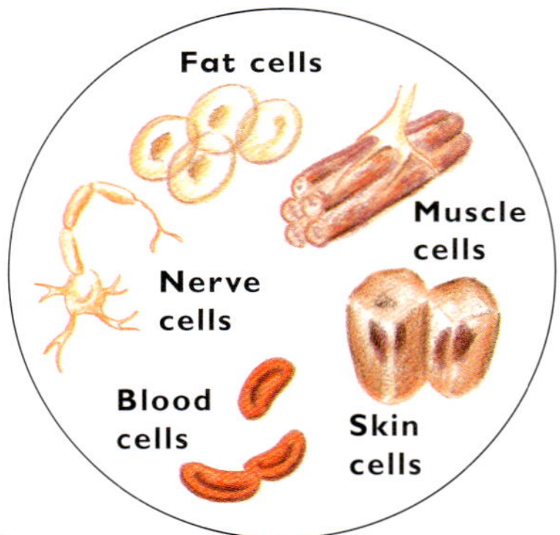

What am I made of?

Your body is made up of millions of tiny cells. You have lots of different kinds of cells. Each kind has a special job to do. Your cells work together to keep you alive.

What can my body do?

All sorts of amazing things! The different parts of your body – both the outside parts and the inside parts like your heart, bones and muscles that you can't see – all work together so you can laugh, cry, walk, talk, jump, hop, run, think, read and sleep!

True or False?

Some people really do look the same.

TRUE. Some twins can be almost identical. You have to look at them closely to tell who is who!

We're mostly made of water.

TRUE. Our bodies are 65% water. The rest is made up of about 50 million million tiny cells.

What's my skin for?

Your skin keeps the insides of your body safe. It helps to keep out water and harmful germs. It also makes sure you don't get too cold or too warm. Your skin grows with you as you grow.

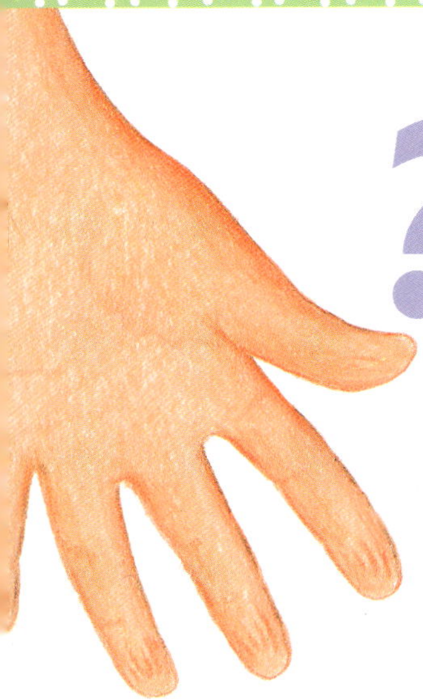

Why do my fingers go wrinkly in the bath?

Your skin contains oil that helps to make it waterproof, like a raincoat. Fingers and toes don't have this oil, so the ends get wrinkly if you stay in water for a long time.

Why do some people have freckles?

Skin contains a special colouring called melanin, which protects it from strong sunlight. Freckles are patches of extra melanin, which can appear on fair skin when it has been in the sun. Dark skin has more melanin than pale skin.

True or False?

Skin can burn.

TRUE. The sun contains harmful rays that can burn your skin. That's why you should always wear sunscreen lotion and a hat on hot, sunny days.

Skin can heal itself.

TRUE. If you cut yourself, your blood dries and makes a scab. New skin grows under the scab, then the scab drops off.

Why do I need haircuts?

Your hair is always growing, that's why! Hair grows quite slowly though, at about 2 mm every week. It grows a bit faster in the summer than in the winter. Hair is made out of keratin. So are your fingernails and toenails.

Why do I get goosebumps?

Your whole body is covered with tiny hairs except on the palms of your hands and the soles of your feet. When you get chilly, little muscles in your skin push the hairs up to trap warm air, and you get goosebumps.

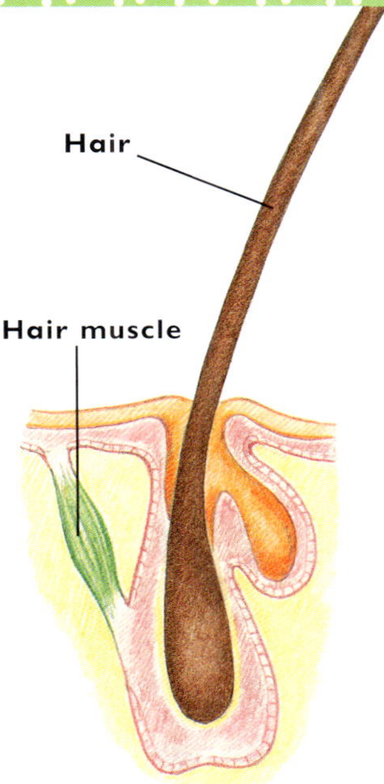

Why is some hair straight and some curly?

Hair grows out of tiny holes in our skin. If the hole is round, then our hair grows straight. If the hole if flat, our hair grows curly.

True or False?

People with fair hair have the most hair.

TRUE. Blond-haired people have about 140,000 hairs on their heads. People with brown, black or red hair have 30,000 to 50,000 fewer.

Your toenails grow faster than your fingernails.

FALSE. Your fingernails grow a little bit faster – about 1 mm in two weeks.

How many bones do I have?

You have about 206 bones in your body, joined together to make a frame called a skeleton. Bones are strong, and some are full of mushy stuff called marrow. Some marrow makes new red blood cells.

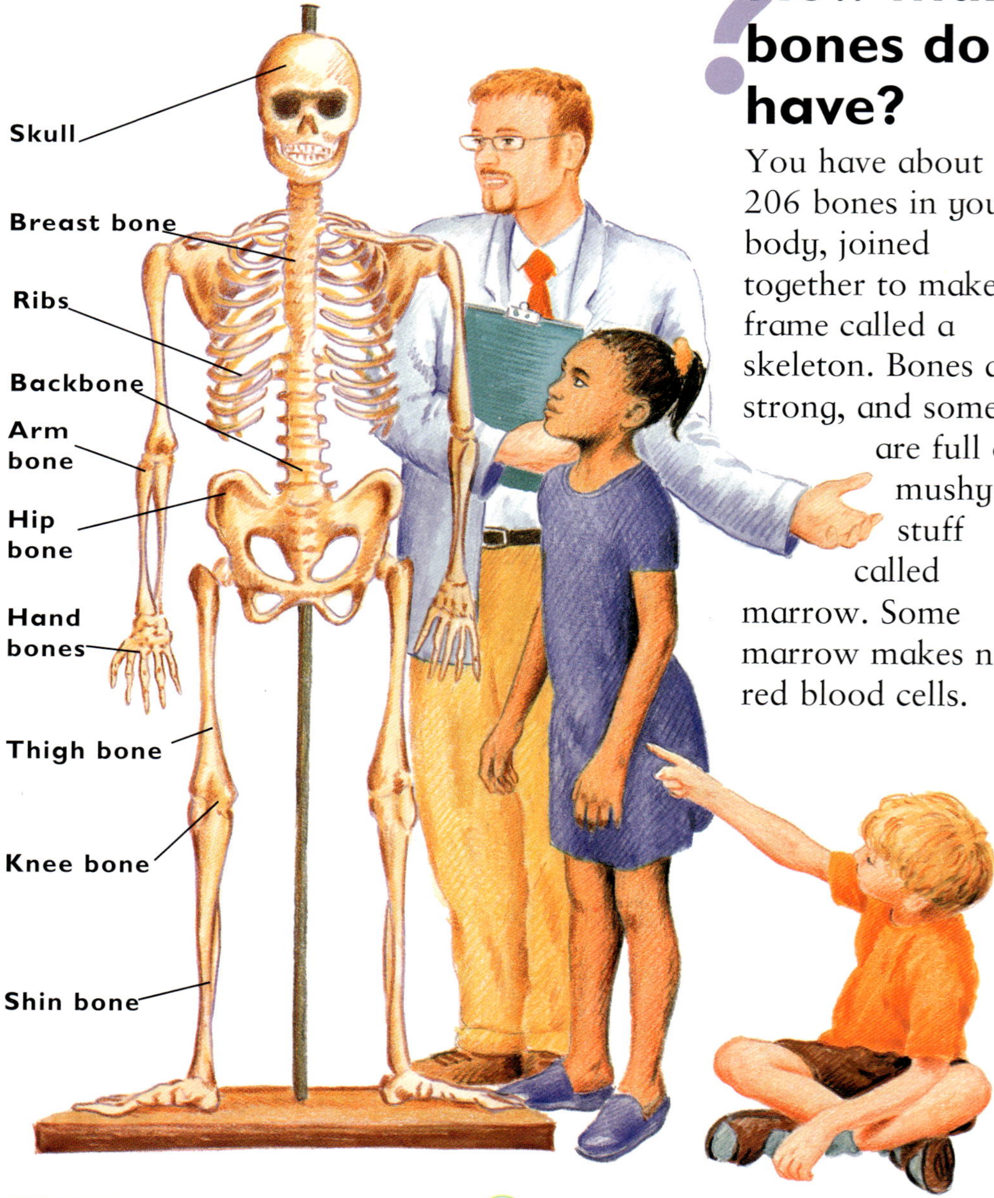

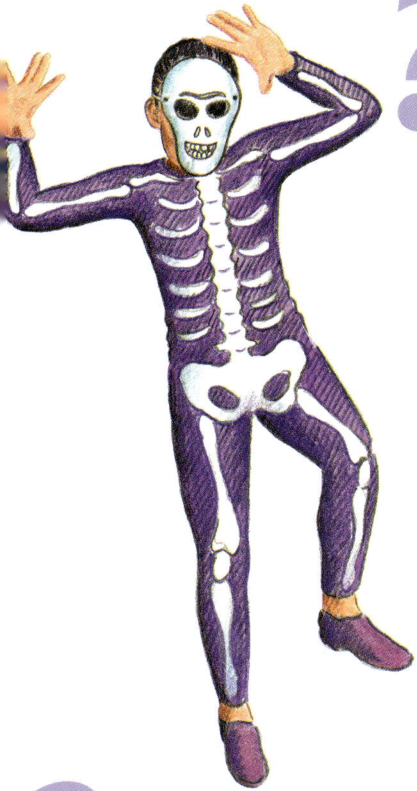

What are bones for?

Bones hold you up. Without them you'd be a floppy jellyfish! Your bones also help to protect the soft parts inside your body – your skull protects your brain, and your ribs protect your heart and lungs. Your bones help you make lots of different movements.

Where is my funny bone?

Your funny bone is on your elbow. It has a big nerve running over it. If you bang it you may feel a strange tingle that can hurt.

True or False?

You shrink a bit every day.

TRUE. You shrink about 1 cm every day because your back bones get squashed together. They stretch out again when you're asleep.

Bones can be broken.

TRUE. Broken bones are wrapped in plaster or plastic while they mend.

What do muscles do?

Muscles help you move. Muscles in your arms lift and pull. Muscles in your thumbs help you to hold things. Muscles in your chest help you to breathe. You have more than 600 muscles to help you move different parts of your body.

How do muscles work?

Muscles are fixed to your bones and usually work in pairs. They tighten to pull a bone one way, and loosen to let the bone move back again.

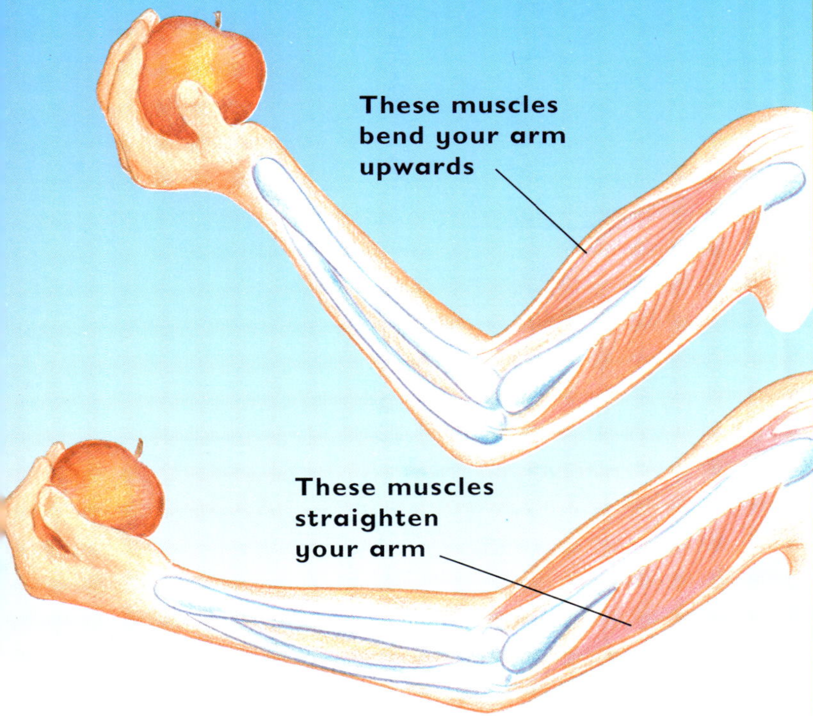

True or False?

Exercises make muscles bigger.

TRUE. Special exercises, such as lifting weights, make muscles bigger and stronger.

It's easier to frown than to smile.

FALSE. Every time you frown, you use 42 muscles in your face. Smiling uses just 17 muscles. Keep smiling!

Where does my food go?

When you eat, food goes down a long tube into your stomach. Juices in your stomach mush the food into a soup then the mush is squeezed through a long, coiled tube called your intestines. There, goodness from the food passes into your blood to be carried all round your body.

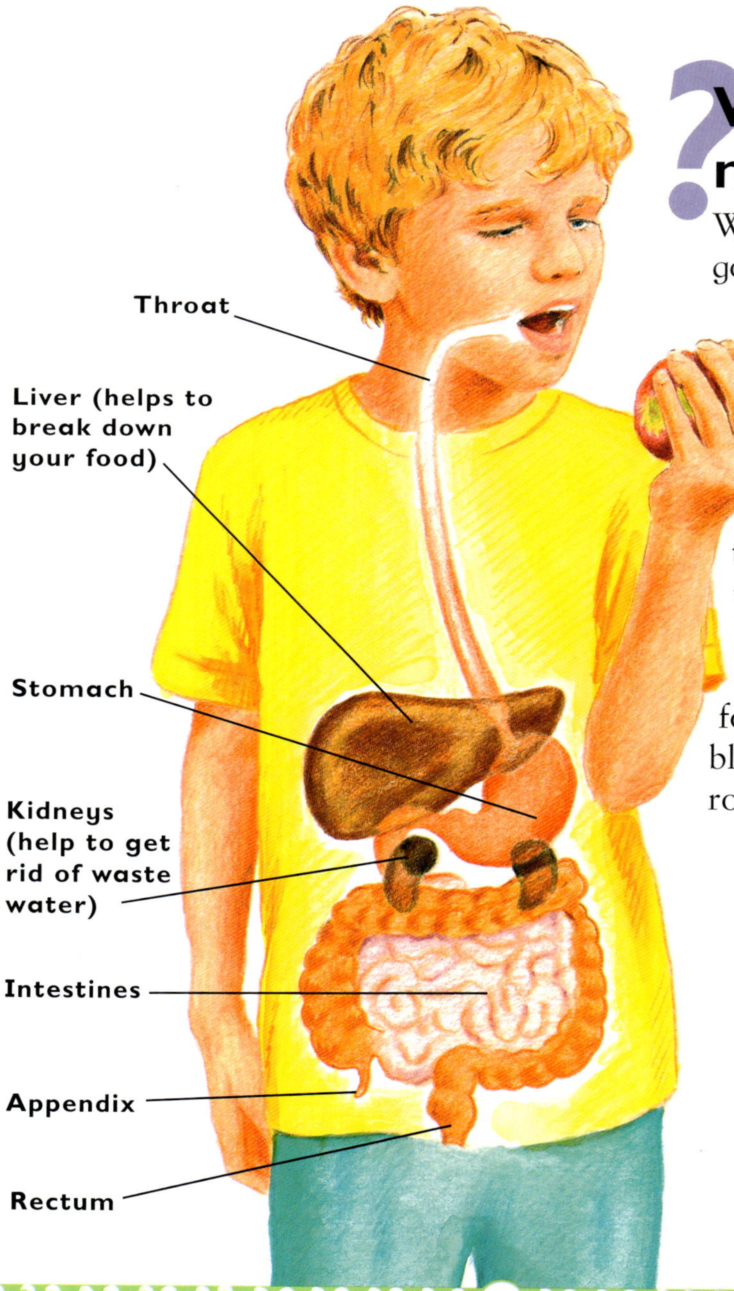

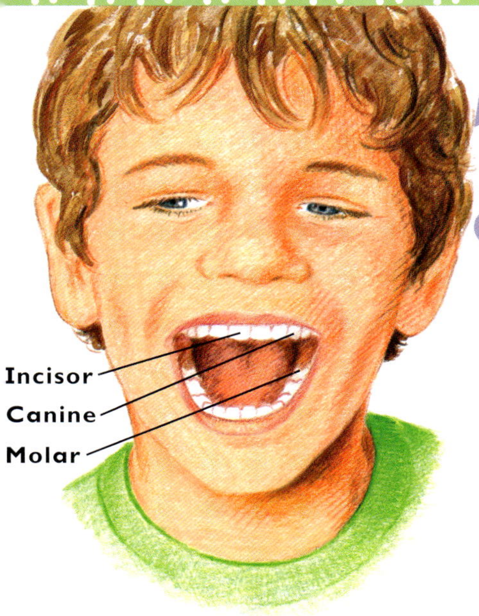

What are teeth for?

Teeth chomp your food into tiny bits so that it's easier to swallow. Sharp incisors cut it up, pointed canines tear it and big molars at the back crush it.

Why do I go to the toilet?

Your body can't use all the food you eat. The bits you don't need pass out of your body as poo. You also go to the toilet to wee. Wee (or urine) is waste water.

True or False?

Teeth fall out.

TRUE. Your first 20 teeth, called milk teeth, fall out as bigger adult teeth push up underneath.

Fizzy drinks can make you burp.

TRUE. Fizzy drinks contain lots of bubbles which go into your tummy. Trapped air rushes up from your tummy and you burp!

What's blood for?

Blood carries oxygen and goodness from the food you eat to all the tiny cells in your body to keep them working properly. It travels around your body in narrow tubes called blood vessels.

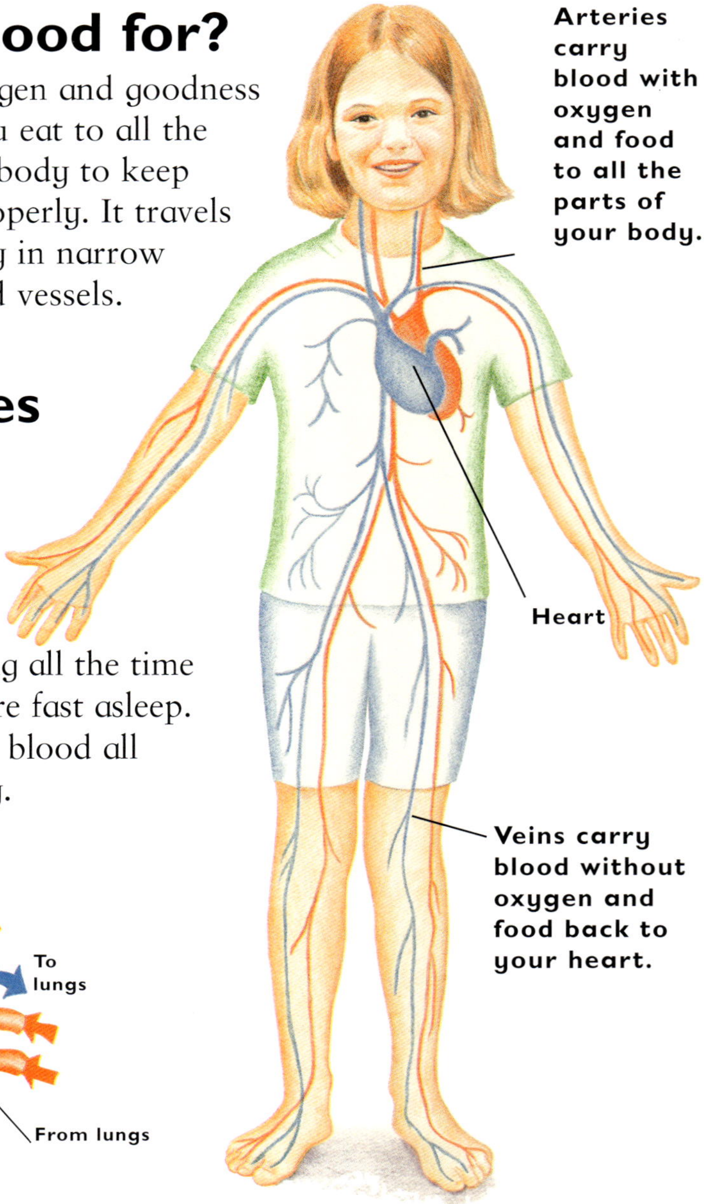

What does my heart do?

Your heart is a special muscle that keeps working all the time – even when you're fast asleep. Its job is to pump blood all around your body.

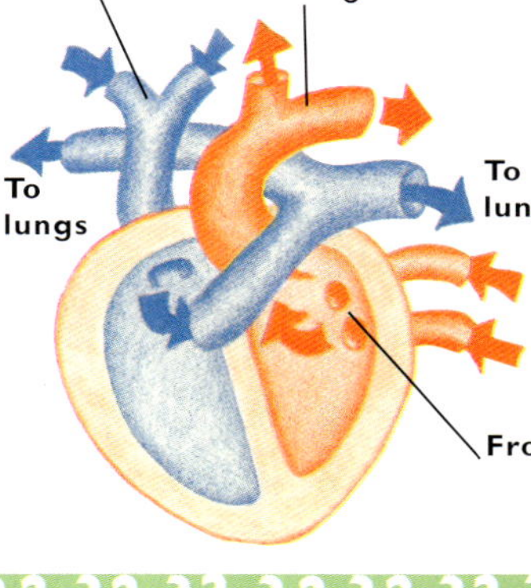

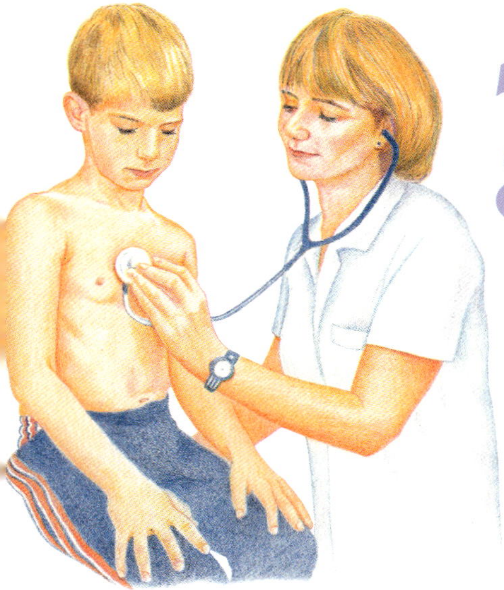

Where's my heart?

Your heart is right in the middle of your chest, just a little bit to the left, between your lungs. It's about as big as your fist.

Can I feel my heart beating?

You can sometimes feel your heart beating in your chest if you've been running fast. Or, if you put your fingers on the inside of your wrist, you can feel the throb of your blood moving in time to your heartbeat.

True or False?

Bruises are really broken blood vessels.

TRUE. Blood leaking from a broken blood vessel turns your skin a bluish colour for a bit until the blood vessel heals.

Running makes your heart beat faster.

TRUE. This helps to push the blood around your body faster so that more blood gets to your muscles to give them energy to work.

What happens when I breathe?

When you breathe in, your chest expands, your lungs get bigger and air goes up your nose, down your windpipe and into your lungs. When you breathe out, your chest and lungs become smaller and your diaphragm arches upwards to squeeze out stale air. All this happens in just a few seconds.

What makes me yawn?

You yawn when you haven't been breathing deeply because you're tired or have been sitting still for a long time and you're not getting enough oxygen to your lungs. To take in more oxygen, you suddenly take a big gulp of air through your mouth.

What do my lungs do?

Your lungs take in a gas called oxygen from the air and pass it into your blood. Your blood carries the oxygen from your lungs to the rest of your body. We need oxygen to stay alive. Your lungs are very large. A grown-up's lungs can hold about three litres of air.

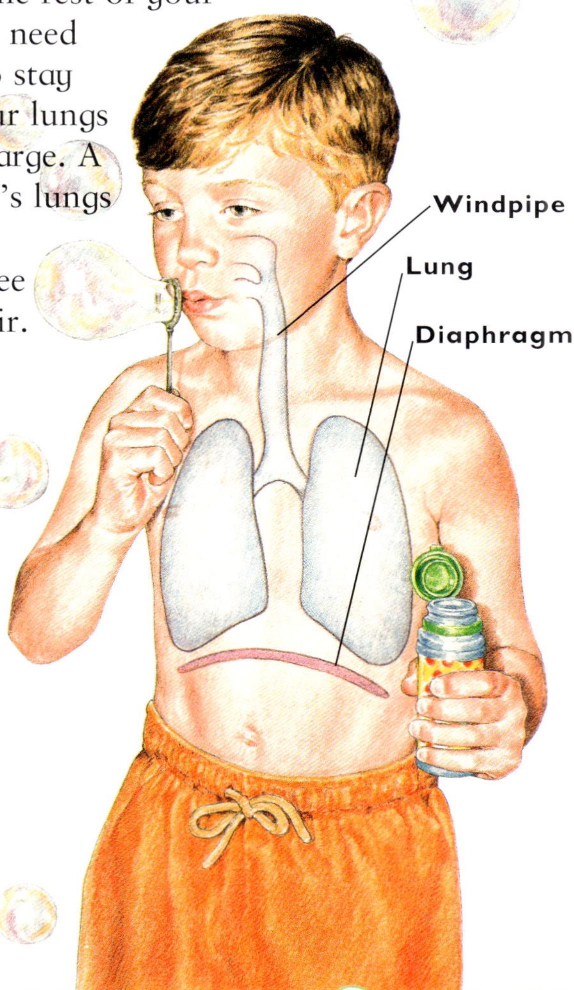

True or False?

Sneezing helps me breathe.

TRUE. Sneezing pushes bits of dust and germs out of your nose so you can breathe properly.

We can breathe underwater.

FALSE. Not unless you've got a tankful of air like a deep-sea diver! There's no air to breathe underwater.

What are nerves?

Nerves carry messages to and from your brain, telling it if you're hungry, hot, cold or in pain. Nerves run from your spinal cord – a thick rope of nerves inside your backbone – to every part of your body.

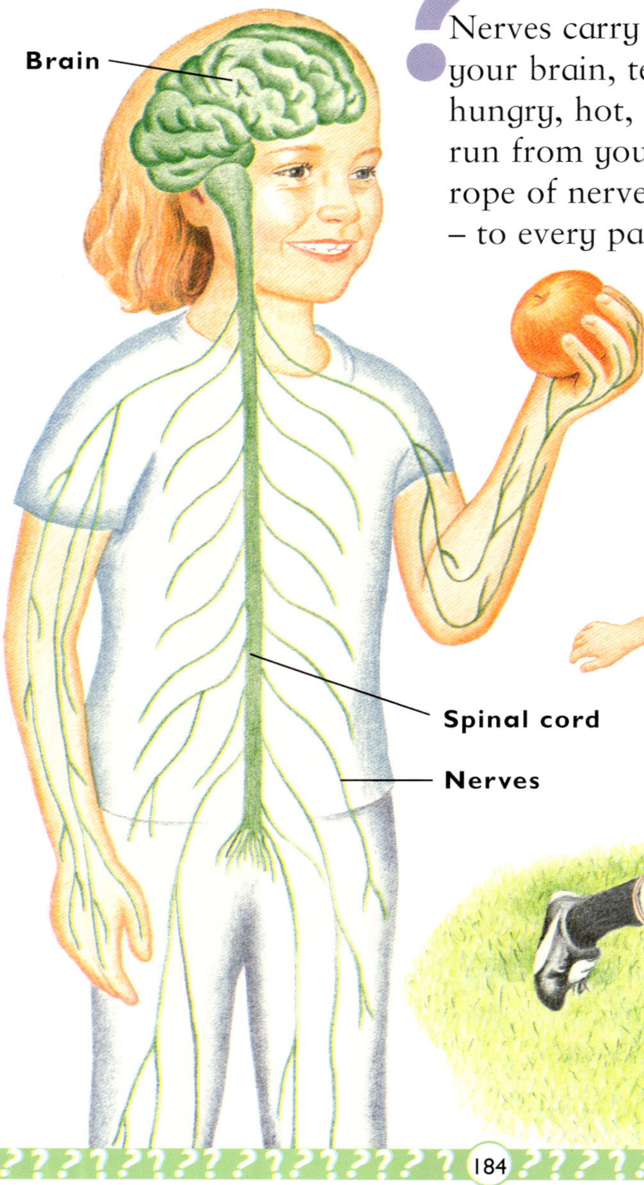

Why do I get pins and needles?

If you lie on your arm or leg for a long time, the tiny nerves in them get squashed. When you move again, the nerves may tingle and throb as they start to work again.

What does my brain do?

Your brain sends signals along your nerves telling your body how to work. It stores all your thoughts and memories and controls everything you do.

True or False?

People with big brains are wise.

FALSE. Your brain is about half the size of your head. A big one doesn't make you wise or clever.

My brain always tells me what to do.

FALSE. If you are in danger, your body can react without your brain telling it to. This is called a reflex action.

How do my eyes help me see?

Each of your eyes is a ball. At the front, there's a black hole called the pupil, which lets in light. Behind the pupil is a lens that helps you to see things close to or far away. The optic nerve carries messages about what you see to your brain.

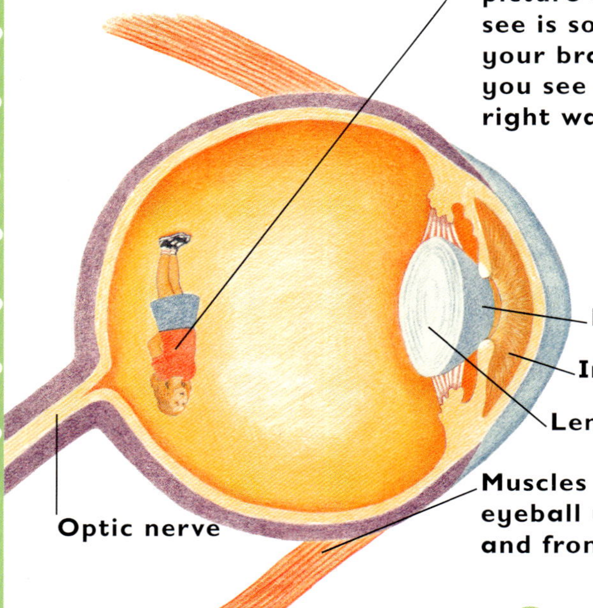

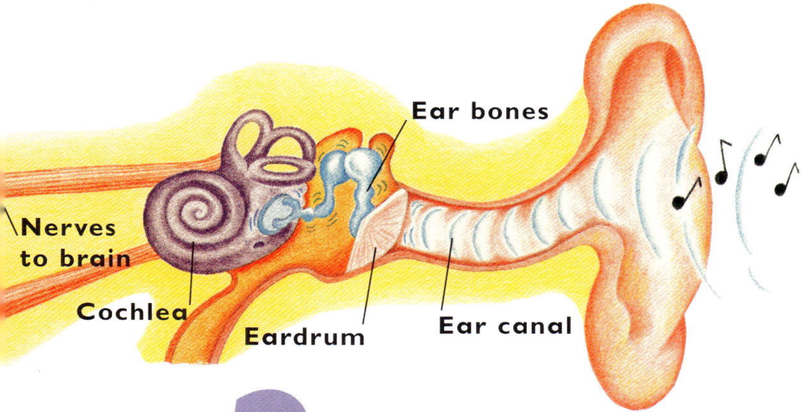

How do my ears help me hear?

The flappy outer parts of your ears collect sounds from the air. The sounds enter your ears as tiny, invisible waves. The waves make your eardrum move up and down, and tiny bones deep inside your ears move, too. Nerves carry sound messages from your ears to your brain.

True or False?

You can hear the sound of the sea in a seashell.

FALSE. What you hear are really the echoes of the sound of your blood moving around inside your head.

Carrots help you see better.

TRUE. Carrots contain special vitamins that might help you to see a little better in the dark.

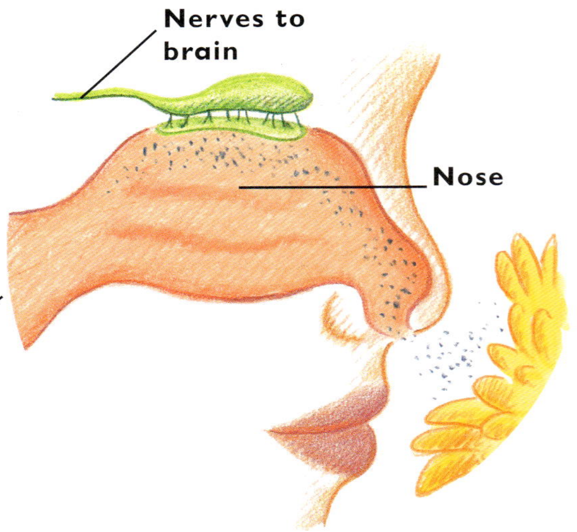

What's my nose for?

Your nose is for smelling things, such as a flower, a tasty snack or stinky rubbish. Tiny bits of food or dirt go up your nose when you breathe in. These bits are too small to see but nerves inside your nose send messages about them to your brain.

Why can't I taste food if I have a cold?

Your sense of smell and taste work together, so if you're eating a crunchy apple, your nose smells how sweet it is and tiny bumps on your tongue (called taste buds) pick up its flavour. When you have a cold, your nose often gets bunged up so it's hard to smell and taste things.

Taste areas of the tongue

True or False?

An ice cream tastes better if you lick it.

TRUE. The tip of your tongue picks out salty things. The sides pick up sour and sweet tastes, and the back picks up bitter tastes, like coffee.

Humans have five senses.

TRUE. Our five senses are touch, taste, smell, sight and hearing.

What is chickenpox?

Chickenpox is a disease, like mumps and measles. It's quite easy to catch but once you've had it you don't usually get it again. Sometimes, we have injections to stop us catching serious diseases that can make us very ill.

Why do I sometimes get sick?

You get sick when tiny harmful germs get into your body. Your white blood cells destroy germs by eating them, so that you get better again.

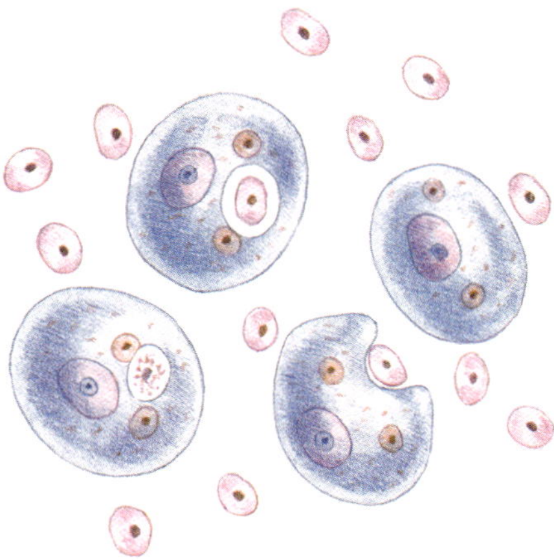

White blood cells eating the invading germs

How do I stay healthy?

To stay healthy, you need to eat food that's good for you, drink lots of water, take plenty of exercise and get lots of sleep.

True or False?

Watching TV is bad for you.

TRUE. If you watch it for several hours a day! TV is fun but everyone needs plenty of exercise like running, swimming or football as well.

Washing gets rid of germs.

TRUE. Germs can get into your body if you rub your eyes or eat with dirty hands, so it's important to keep your hands clean and always wash them before a meal.

Where did I come from?

You began when a sperm from your father joined with an egg from your mother. A cell formed and began to make more and more cells and a baby – YOU – began to grow. A baby grows inside its mother's womb for nine months.

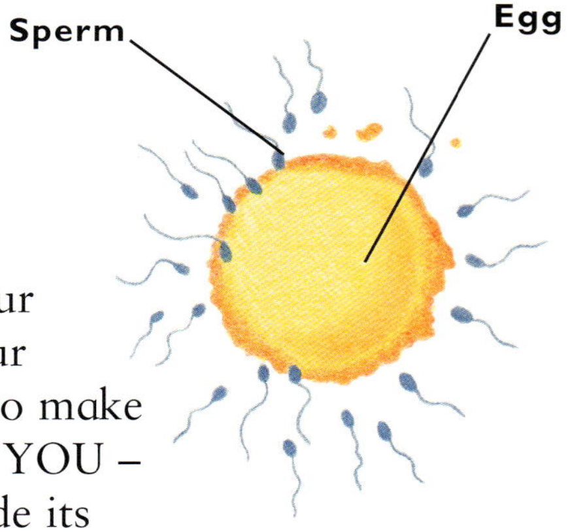

Two months

The baby's heart is beating.

Six months

The baby weighs as much as a bag of sugar. It may suck its thumb.

Seven months

The baby can swallow and hear and recognise its mother's voice.

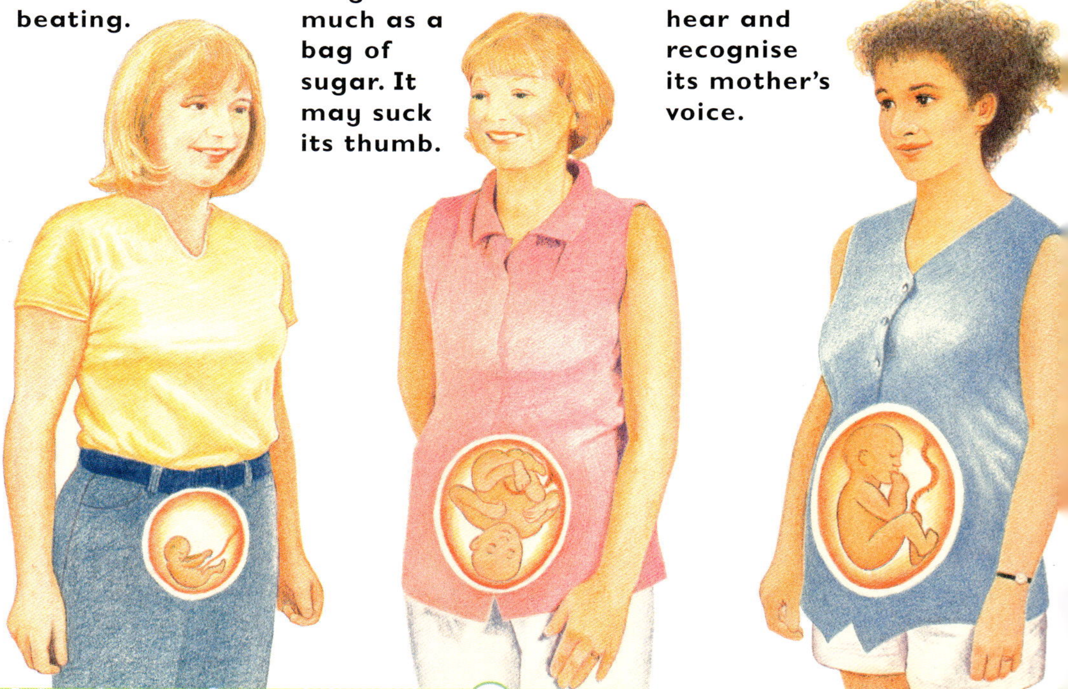

What's my tummy button?

Your tummy button, or your navel, is the place where you were once joined to your mother by a cord called the umbilical cord when you were inside her womb. You got all the food and oxygen you needed to grow through this cord.

Nine months

At nine months, the baby is plump and strong and nearly ready to be born. It is around 50 cm long and weighs around 3.4 kg.

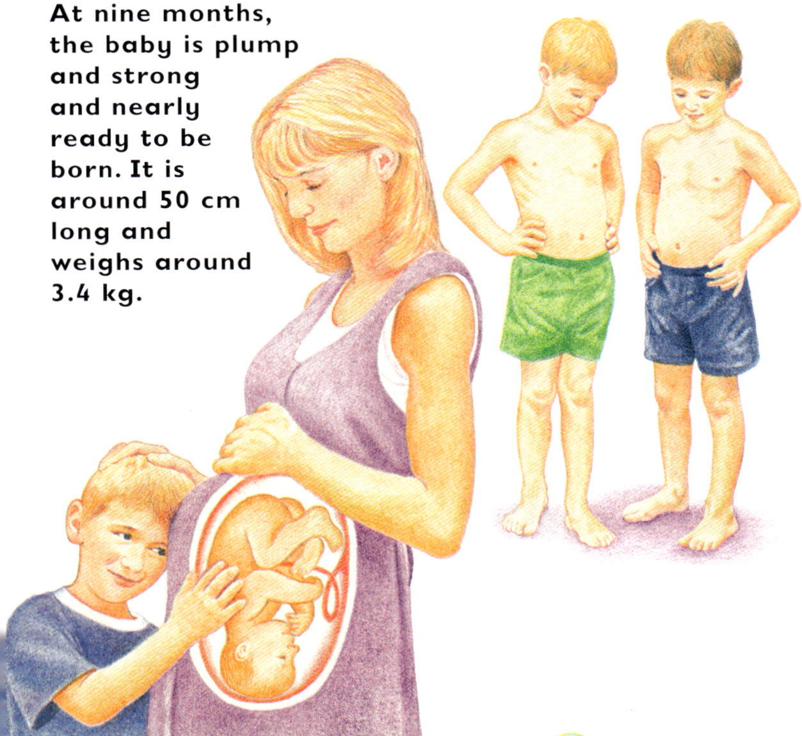

True or False?

You are still growing.

TRUE. You get taller and stronger and you carry on changing shape, until you're about 18 years old.

Some mothers have more than one baby at a time.

TRUE. Two babies are called twins, four are called quad-ruplets and six babies are called sextuplets.

Why do I sleep?

You need to sleep to stay healthy. While you're asleep, your body is resting, growing and repairing itself, getting ready for another busy day, and your brain is sorting out your thoughts.

Why do I dream?

Dreams are times during the night when you sleep lightly. Everyone has about five dreams a night but we don't always remember them. Scary dreams are called nightmares. Some are so frightening, they may wake you up.

What's sleepwalking?

Sleepwalking is when someone gets out of bed and walks around when they're still fast asleep. Sleepwalking is quite rare, and no one knows why some people do it.

True or False?

Adults need more sleep than children.

FALSE. Children need more sleep than grown-ups, because they're still growing and their brains have new information to sort out and store away.

Your brain carries on working while you're asleep.

TRUE. So do your heart and lungs, but they all work more slowly than when you are awake.

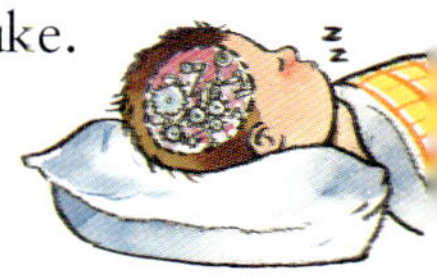

Which animals have scaly skin?

and other questions about types of animals

What do a mosquito and an elephant have in common?

Although they are very different in shape and size, a mosquito and an elephant have something in common. They are both animals! Animals are living, breathing things that can move around to find food, shelter or a mate.

Which plant is really an animal?

Despite their name sea cucumbers are animals, not plants. Their shape and knobbly skin make them look a bit like a cucumber. But unlike cucumber plants, they can move around.

Sea cucumber

What are the simplest life-forms?

Protozoa are tiny life-forms, which don't have muscles like animals, but aren't plants or fungi either.

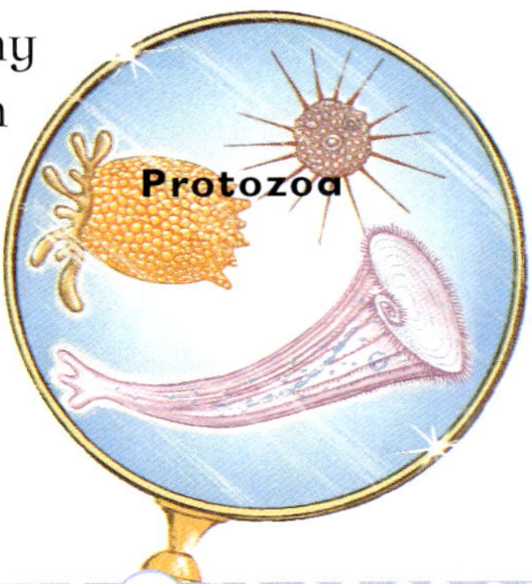

True or False?

The only life-forms on Earth are animals.

FALSE. Plants and fungi are alive. We know this because they grow and reproduce to make copies of themselves.

All animals need sunshine.

FALSE. At the bottom of the deepest ocean, where it is cold and totally dark, there are tubeworms and other strange creatures.

Which animals are spineless?

About 90 per cent of all the animals on Earth have no backbone, or spine. They are called invertebrates and range from snails to big, wobbly jellyfish. All invertebrates are cold-blooded – their body temperature is the same as the air or water around them.

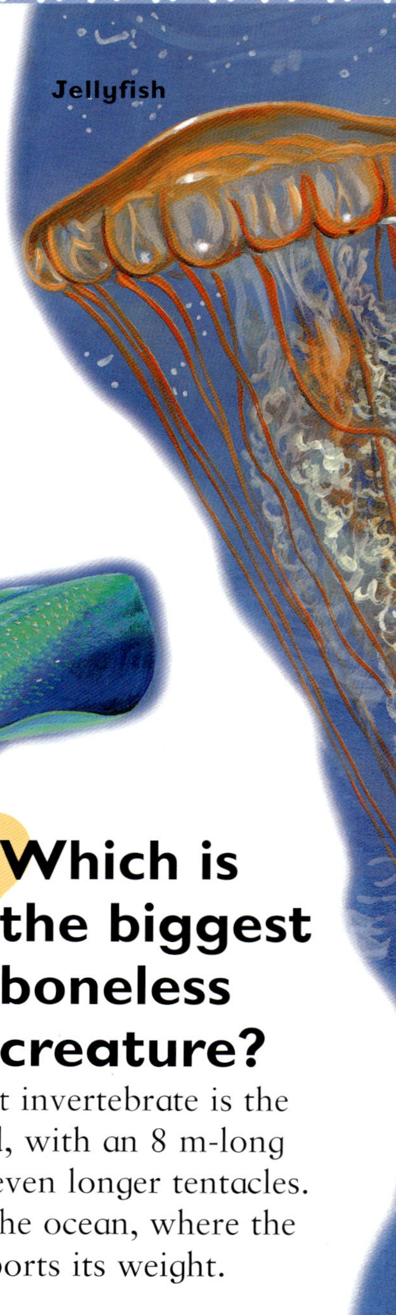

Which is the biggest boneless creature?

The biggest invertebrate is the giant squid, with an 8 m-long body and even longer tentacles. It lives in the ocean, where the water supports its weight.

Do worms have a skeleton?

Earthworms are invertebrates – they do not have a spine or any other bones. But they do have water-filled tubes, which run along the length of their bodies and act a bit like a skeleton.

True or False?

Snails and oysters are closely related.

TRUE. Oysters and snails have soft bodies and shells. They both belong to a family of animals known as molluscs.

Starfish have five arms.

FALSE. Most do, but some have as many as 50! The arms are called 'rays', because they spread out like rays from the Sun.

What sort of animal is a lobster?

The lobster is a type of invertebrate called a crustacean. Crustaceans have shells (crusts) and lots of jointed legs. A lobster has five pairs of legs, with claws on its front ones to grip and stab prey.

Who wears armour at the bottom of the sea?

The tough outer shell of a lobster or crab is like a suit of armour, stopping hungry fish and other predators from biting the animal's body. Most crabs live on the seabed, eating rotting remains that sink down there.

Lobster

How do crabs grow bigger?

Our skin stretches as we grow, but a hard shell can't stretch. When a crab grows too big for its shell, it gets rid of it. The new shell underneath is soft at first, but soon hardens. A crab may do this as many as 20 times in its life.

Crab losing shell

True or False?

Crustaceans can only live in the water.

FALSE. Most crustaceans live in or around water, but land crabs and woodlice live on land. Even so, they prefer to live in damp places.

Some crabs steal shells.

TRUE. Hermit crabs don't grow their own shells. They find an old empty shell and hide their long, soft body in there instead!

Stag beetle

Which animals have a skeleton on the outside?

The tough casing that protects a beetle's body is called an exoskeleton. A crab's shell is a type of exoskeleton, too. Most invertebrates rely on an outside skeleton to protect their boneless body.

Are spiders insects?

Spiders aren't insects, because they have too many legs and too few body parts! An insect has six legs and three parts to its body (head, thorax and abdomen). A spider has eight legs and its head and thorax are joined.

Dragonfly

Tarantula spider

Can insects fly?

The ones with wings can! Butterflies, bees and midges are flying insects that have two pairs of wings. Houseflies make do with a single pair. Some insects called termites break off their wings on purpose, when they don't need them anymore.

True or False?

Centipedes have 100 feet.

FALSE. 'Centipede' means 100 feet, but some centipedes have more than 350 feet! All the better for chasing after prey!

Scorpions are closely related to spiders.

TRUE. If you count a scorpion's walking legs, you'll soon see the family resemblance. Both spiders and scorpions have eight.

How do fish breathe?

Fish have slits called gills on the sides of their heads, that allow them to get oxygen from water, just as we get oxygen from air. All fish breathe using gills.

How do salmon leap?

Salmon leap if they meet a mini waterfall when they are heading up-river to breed. The strong, muscly tails that they use for swimming also help to thrust them up into the air.

Hammerhead shark

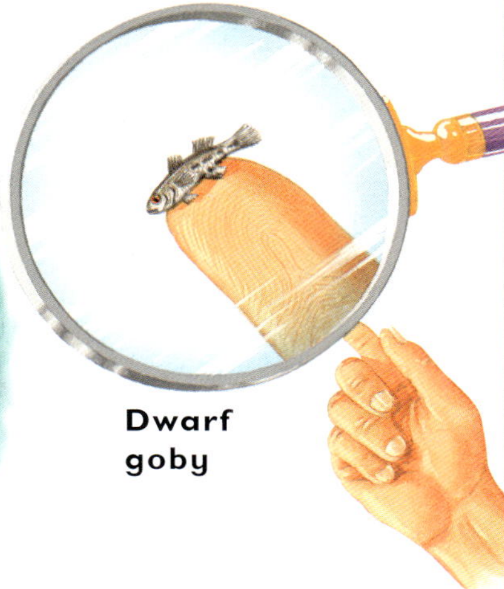

Dwarf goby

Which fish would fit on your fingertip?

The dwarf goby is the tiniest fish in the world, at about 1 cm long. The whale shark is biggest – it's about 12 m long from nose to tail, but quite harmless to people.

True or False?

Whales are a type of fish.

FALSE. Whales and dolphins are warm-blooded mammals, which come up for air. Fish are cold-blooded and breathe underwater.

Oarfish are as long as an oar.

FALSE. Unless it was a giant's boat! Oarfish are as long as four canoes in a row.

Why are frogs slimy?

A frog's thin, slimy skin allows it to absorb oxygen from both air and water. Frogs are amphibians, animals that start life in water, but gradually change so they can survive on land, too.

How can you tell a frog from a toad?

Most frogs have smooth skin, but toads are warty! Frogs and toads are the only amphibians that lose their tail and grow strong back legs for jumping.

Which is the weirdest amphibian?

The axolotl never really grows up! It breeds when it is still at 'tadpole' stage and only changes into an adult body if its pond dries up and it is forced to live on land.

True or False?

If you kiss a frog, it will magically turn into a prince.

FALSE. It's not a good idea to kiss frogs or toads, because some of them ooze poison.

The goliath frog is the biggest amphibian.

FALSE. The goliath is as long as a ruler, and the biggest frog, but the Chinese giant salamander is nearly four times as long.

Tortoise

Which animals have scaly skin?

Snakes, lizards, crocodiles and turtles have dry, scaly skin. These cold-blooded creatures belong to a family of animals called reptiles. There are about 6,000 types of reptile.

How long do tortoises live?

Tortoises are the longest-living animals on Earth. Some probably live beyond their 200th birthday! Perhaps it's because their tough, bony shell protects them from dangerous predators.

Green python

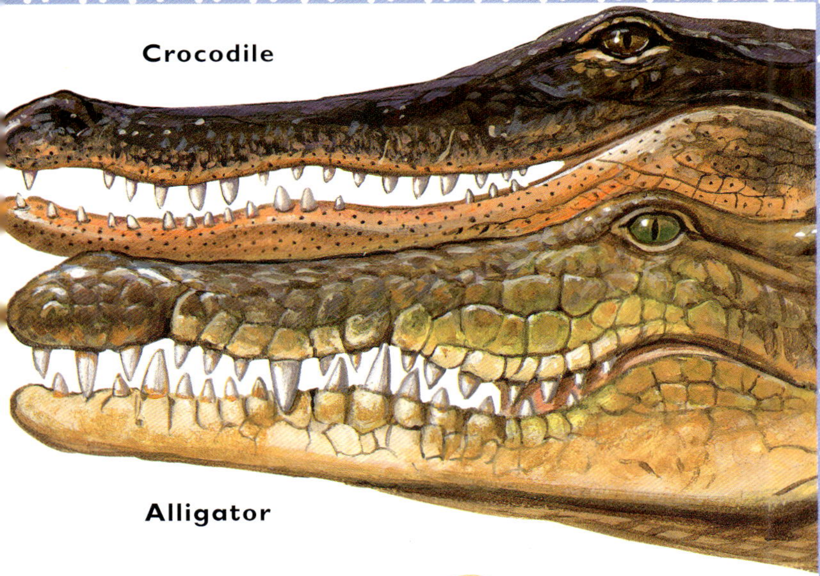

How can you tell a crocodile from an alligator?

You can tell them apart by their smile. When a crocodile's mouth is shut, you can still see one of its bottom teeth poking out.

True or False?

Thread snakes are the longest snakes by far.

FALSE. Thread snckes are the shortest snakes at about 10 cm. Pythons are the longest – they can grow to 10 m!

Snakes aren't able to blink.

TRUE. They can't blink, because they don't have any eyelids! A see-through scale protects each of their eyes.

Why do birds have feathers?

Soft, downy feathers keep birds' bodies toasty and warm, while waxy outer ones keep off the rain. Most importantly, feathers allow birds to fly. Birds beat their feathered wings to lift off the ground and fly through the air.

Parrots

Penguins

Can all birds swim?

No, but some can. Penguins have webbed feet, stubby wings, oily waterproof feathers, and a layer of fat to keep them warm.

Why do eagles have such hooked beaks?

An eagle's hooked beak is perfect for tearing up meat. Herons have long beaks for spearing fish. Macaws have powerful beaks for cracking nuts.

Bald eagle

True or False?

All birds fly.

FALSE. Not all birds need to fly! Penguins swim instead, while ostriches, emus, rheas and kiwis all run away from their enemies.

Birds can't fly backwards.

FALSE. Hummingbirds are the only birds which fly backwards. It helps them to hover around a flower filled with nectar.

Which animals have fur?

Animals that have fur are called mammals. The other things that mammals have in common are having a backbone, breathing air, being warm-blooded and feeding their babies on milk. The mammal family includes bears and monkeys, bats and mice.

Bear and cubs

Porcupine

Are all mammals soft to touch?

Not the spiny porcupine! Although it is related to rats and mice and does have fur, the porcupine also has lots of spiky quills to protect it from its enemies.

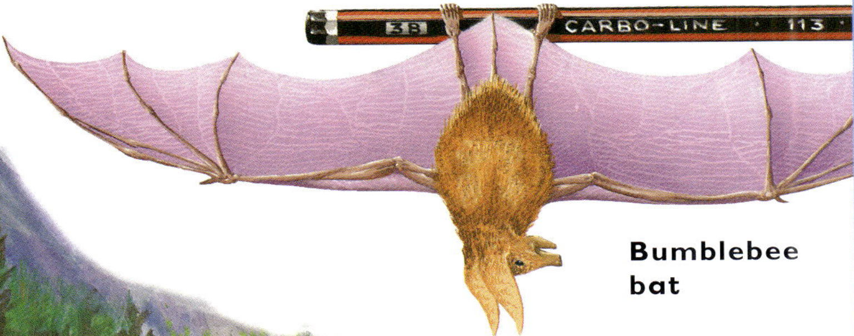

Bumblebee bat

Which is the tiniest mammal?

The smallest mammal is the bumblebee bat that lives in caves in Thailand. The bat's body is only about 3 cm long. Its wingspan is much longer – about 14 cm!

True or False?

All mammals live on land.

FALSE. Manatees, seals and whales live in water. They have flippers and tails, not arms and legs.

Humans are mammals.

TRUE. Hair is a type of fur, and we feed our babies on milk. Humans are primates, like chimps and gorillas.

Koala and young

What type of animal is a koala?

Along with kangaroos, koalas belong to a group of mammals called marsupials. Tiny baby koalas live in their mother's pouch, where they can feed on her milk for the first seven months of their life.

Duckbilled platypus

Which mammal lays eggs?

Unlike most mammals, the duckbilled platypus lays eggs that hatch after about ten days. The mother feeds her babies on milk, until they are big enough to hunt for fish.

Do all mammals breathe through the mouth?

No – whales breathe through a blowhole on the top of their head. When they surface, warm breath pushes out. Out in the cold, it makes a misty spout that can be as high as 12 m!

True or False?

Marsupials only live in Australia.

FALSE. Koalas, wombats, possums and kangaroos live in Australia. Opossums live in North and South America.

Only two types of mammal can lay eggs.

TRUE. The platypus and echidna lay eggs. Echidna mums keep their eggs in their pouch, where the babies hatch and drink milk.

Gecko

Which lizard looks like a tree trunk?

The leaf-tailed gecko's speckled skin blends in perfectly with the trunk of a tree. So long as this reptile keeps still, its clever camouflage stops any predator from noticing it.

Why are zebras stripy?

Black and white stripes confuse lions and other predators. The stripes seem to wobble in the heat haze. Each zebra has its own pattern, so stripes might also help foals find their mum in the herd.

Zebras

Who wears two fur coats?

Some mammals change their coat to match the season, including the hares, foxes and wolves of the snowy north. Their brown coat turns white in winter for camouflage against the snow. It also grows extra-thick to keep out the cold.

Arctic fox

Arctic hares

True or False?

Young zebra foals are black and white.

FALSE. The foal's stripes start out brown. They darken as the zebra grows. Finally they turn black.

Butterflies have eyes on their wings.

TRUE. Not for seeing with, but spots that look like huge eyes, to scare off predators.

Ostrich

Do turtles lay eggs in the sea?

Turtles spend all their lives out at sea, but the mums come ashore to lay their leathery eggs. When the eggs hatch, the baby turtles crawl out of the sand and head straight down to the water.

Which bird lays the biggest egg?

The biggest bird lays the biggest egg! An ostrich is much taller than an adult human, and its eggs are giant, too. A single ostrich egg weighs more than 22 chicken eggs!

Do tree frogs lay eggs in trees?

Like all frogs, tiny tree frogs need to lay their eggs in water. They use pools of rainwater cupped in the leaves of rainforest trees. There's fresh rain every day, so there's little danger of the eggs drying out.

Tree frog

Baby turtles

True or False?

Some fish keep their eggs in their mouths.

TRUE. Eggs left alone to hatch are often eaten by other animals. Cichlids keep their eggs safe and sound in their mouths.

The smallest bird egg of all is less than 1 cm in length.

TRUE. The egg of the vervain hummingbird is tiny – about the same size as a pea!

Which dad has babies?

After seahorses mate, the male carries the eggs in a pouch. When it's time for the eggs to hatch, hundreds of tiny seahorses squirt out! Seahorses get their name because their head looks a bit like a horse's – but really they are fish! They have fins and a tail, and they breathe through gills.

Which baby bounces along?

A baby kangaroo, or joey, has a very bouncy ride in its mum's pouch as she hops around. The joey is only about 2 cm long when it is born. It crawls up through its mum's fur into her pouch and stays there, drinking her milk. The joey only leaves the cosy pouch when it is about nine months old.

Kangaroo

True or False?

Butterflies can fly the minute they hatch.

FALSE. Butterfly eggs hatch into hungry caterpillars. They only change into their adult form later.

Cuckoos are the best mums in the world.

FALSE. Cuckoos lay their eggs in another bird's nest, and let it keep the egg warm and feed the chick!

Great White shark

How well do sharks smell?

Sharks smell very well! As a shark swims, water flows in and out of its nose. If the shark picks up the scent of blood it makes a beeline for it, 'sniffing' hard to stay on course.

Hares

Why do rabbits have big ears?

Rabbits and hares have enormous ears for their size – and super hearing. The twitchy, outsize ears funnel the sound. Big ears also allow heat to escape, so the animals stay cool.

How do eagles find their prey?

By sight – like all birds of prey, eagles have keen eyesight. A golden eagle can spot a rabbit's slightest movement on the ground from 2 km away!

True or False?

Ducks have see-through eyelids.

TRUE. See-through eyelids protect the ducks' eyes underwater, but still let the ducks see when they're diving for food.

Spiders aren't able to see.

FALSE. But their eyesight is bad. The jumping spider is best, but it can only see as far as the end of a ruler!

Why are jungles in danger?

and other questions about things that grow

Where do plants live?

Plants live everywhere! They grow in towns and cities, in the countryside, in streams, lakes and rivers, and by the sea. Some plants can live where we cannot. Cacti survive in hot, dry deserts, and some tiny flowering plants live at the top of freezing cold mountains.

How many kinds of plants are there?

There are around 400,000 different kinds of plants. They come in all sorts of shapes and sizes from tiny lichens that grow on rocks, beautiful flowers, and towering trees that reach towards the sky.

True or False?

Plants live in the sea.

TRUE. Marine, or sea, plants include lots of different kinds of seaweed, such as kelp and sea lettuce.

Trees are the biggest plants.

TRUE. Coast redwood trees in California, USA, are the tallest plants in the world. They can grow more than 100 m high.

What is a plant?

A plant is a living thing, just like you. Like all living things, plants grow, breathe, feed and make babies. Unlike animals, green plants can use their leaves, roots, stems and flowers to make the food they need to grow. Mushrooms and other fungi aren't plants because they don't need sunlight to grow.

Why do plants have roots?

A plant needs roots to hold it in the soil so that it doesn't blow over in the wind. Tall trees need longer, stronger roots than small flowering plants. Roots also suck up water from the soil and carry it up the trunk or stem to the rest of the plant.

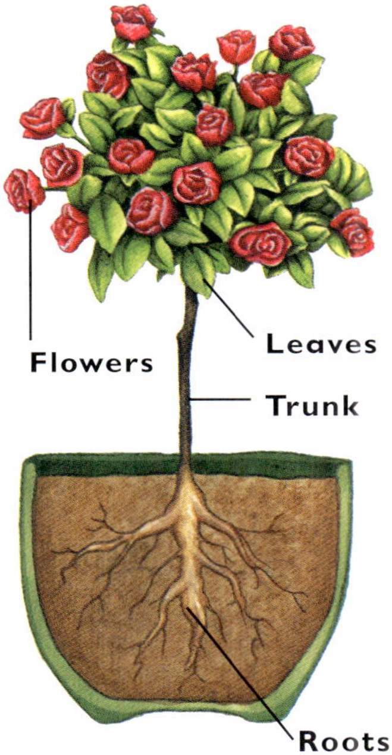

What do plants need to grow?

Plants need sunlight, water, air and space to grow. Most plants will die if they are left in the dark or uprooted from damp soil.

True or False?

Every plant has roots in the soil.

FALSE. Some plants grow on other plants, not in the soil. These plants are called epiphytes. They include beautiful orchid flowers.

Plants are able to move.

TRUE. Plants don't walk or run but they do move as they grow. Some climbing plants twist around other plants as they grow upwards.

Why do plants have leaves?

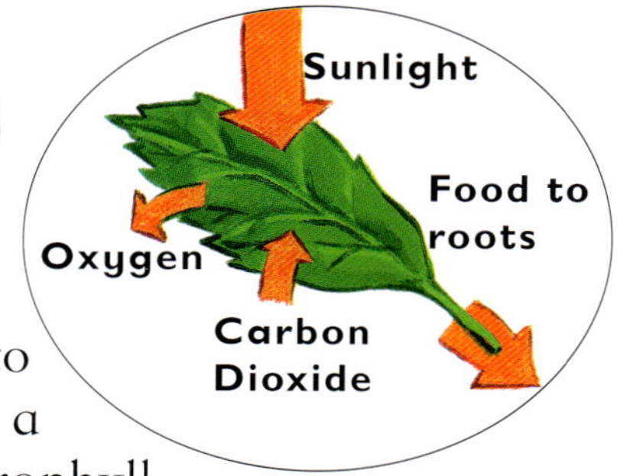

Because leaves work hard, making food for the plant to grow. Green leaves contain a green colouring called chlorophyll. The chlorophyll uses sunlight and a gas from the air, called carbon dioxide, to change water into a kind of sugar. The sugar feeds the plant. This way of making food is called photosynthesis.

Why do some leaves change colour in the autumn?

Green leaves change colour when their green colouring, or chlorophyll, breaks down. Other colours then show through and the leaves look brown, red or yellowy gold.

Why do plants have stems?

Stems grow towards the sunlight and support the plants' leaves, so that they can make food. Stems also carry water, minerals and sugary food (called sap) around the plant. Some plants have straight stems, others are curly.

True or False?

All trees have leaves.

FALSE. The saguaro cactus is a leafless tree. Instead of leaves, it has chlorophyll in its thick, green stems, which make food and store water.

Plants sweat.

TRUE. During photosynthesis, plants give off water. Just look at the water on the windows of a greenhouse!

Why do trees lose their leaves?

Some trees lose their leaves in the wintertime when there is less sunlight and water freezes in the ground. These trees, called deciduous trees, rest during the winter. They store enough food during the summer to keep themselves alive until the following spring when new leaves grow.

What are growing rings?

A growing ring is added to a tree's trunk every year. The ring is thick if the tree has grown a lot during a warm, long summer with plenty of rain, and thin if the tree has not grown much because the weather has been harsh.

Do all trees lose their leaves?

No – some trees keep their leaves all year round. They are called evergreens because they are always, or forever, green. They include spruces and pine trees.

True or False?

Plants sleep.

TRUE. Green plants can only make food during the day when there's lots of sunlight. At night, they shut down and have a rest.

Some trees are ancient.

TRUE. The giant sequoia can live for over 2,000 years. Some bristlecone pines are over 4,500 years old! They're the world's oldest trees.

Why do plants have flowers?

Most plants have colourful flowers to attract birds, bats and lots of different kinds of insects, such as beetles, butterflies and bees. These animals help the plants make seeds to grow new plants.

Why do flowers smell?

Sweet-smelling flowers help to attract animals. The scent tells insects and other animals that the flower contains a sweet, sugary juice called nectar which the animals like to drink.

How are seeds made?

Flowers have male parts called stamens and female parts called carpels. The stamens make tiny grains of pollen. The carpels contain eggs, called ovules. Seeds are made when the pollen reaches the ovules. This is called pollination.

True or False?

All flowers smell sweet.

FALSE. The rafflesia plant smells like rotten meat! This attracts flies that like pongy smells.

Some flowers open at night.

TRUE. The evening primrose opens its petals at night and lets out a sweet scent to attract night-flying moths.

How do insects help flowers?

Insects help to pollinate flowers by carrying pollen from the carpels of one flower to the ovules of another flower. When a bee feeds on the sweet nectar in a flower, pollen sticks to the bee's furry body. The pollen brushes off on to the next flower visited by the bee.

Why do some birds drink from flowers?

Some birds like to drink nectar, too. The hummingbird sucks up nectar through its long straw-like beak. As it feeds, its head brushes against the flower's pollen grains.

Which flowers do bats like?

Some bats like to feed on the bird of paradise flower. The part of the plant that makes pollen is flat for the bat to perch on.

True or False?

Pollen is tiny.

TRUE. Pollen grains are so small that 50 or so would fit on the head of a pin!

All plants need animals for pollination.

FALSE. Some plants, such as goosegrass, pollinate themselves. Sometimes the wind blows dry pollen on to the female parts of nearby plants. This happens with most grasses and trees.

How many seeds are in each fruit?

Some fruits, such as peaches, mangoes and avocadoes, contain just one large seed inside a hard stone. Other fruits, such as oranges, lemons, apples and pears, contain several seeds called pips. Berries have lots of tiny pips around the outside of each fruit.

How do plants look after their seeds?

Many seeds have hard coats or cases to protect them as they grow. Some plants also have tasty, colourful fruits growing around their seeds. Animals eat the seeds along with the fruit. This helps to spread the seeds.

Inside an avocado

True or False?

Tomatoes are vegetables.

FALSE. Many people think that tomatoes, cucumbers and peas are vegetables but they are really fruit because they all contain seeds.

Nuts are seeds.

TRUE. Nuts are seeds covered by a hard or spiky shell.

Which seeds can fly?

Some small, light seeds float in the air. Sycamore seeds have wings. Dandelion seeds have tiny parachutes. Other seeds are round and heavy so that they drop to the ground and roll away from their parent to get enough space to grow.

How do animals help to spread seeds?

When animals eat fruit they may spit out the seeds or the seeds pass through the animal and fall to the ground as droppings. Sometimes seeds with tiny hooks or spines stick to an animal's fur and are carried a long way before they fall.

True or False?

Plants explode.

TRUE. Some plants, such as poppies or honesty, have seed case pods. The pods explode, sending the seeds flying.

Seeds can float.

TRUE. Coconut seeds drop into the sea and sail a long way to reach land. Each big seed contains food for a new coconut plant to grow.

What do seeds need?

Like large plants, seeds need light, air, water and space to grow. Seeds mostly grow in spring, when the soil warms in the sun and there is plenty of rain. Some seeds are planted on purpose by people to grow flowers, fruit and vegetables.

How do seeds grow?

The seed swells up in damp soil until its seed case bursts. A tiny root then pushes down into the soil and a thin shoot pushes up towards the light. When a seed starts to grow, we say it germinates.

Which plants are fun to grow?

Marigolds, nasturtiums, peas, beansprouts and mustard and cress are all easy and fun to grow from seeds. You can even grow a plant from a carrot top!

True or False?

Roots grow from seeds first of all.

TRUE. Roots grow first to take in water from the soil. Shoots and stems then grow from the other end of the seed.

Seeds need to grow quickly.

FALSE. Some seeds that grow in the desert can wait years for the rains to come before they can grow.

Do all plants have seeds?

Many flowering plants use their seeds to spread but some also use their bulbs, roots or stems. Daffodil and tulip bulbs make lots of tiny baby bulbs. Each bulb produces a new flower. Tubers and rhizomes are underground roots or stems swollen with food. We eat some tubers, such as potato and carrot tubers.

Which plants have runners?

Plants such as wild strawberries have long stems called runners that stretch down into the soil. New roots and shoots grow from each runner then the runner rots away.

What are spores?

Spores are tiny, dust-like specks made by lichens, mosses or ferns. These plants don't have flowers or seeds. Instead, the spores fly away to make new plants.

True or False?

You can eat some bulbs.

TRUE. Onions and garlic are two kinds of bulb you can eat. But other bulbs, such as daffodils and tulips, would poison you.

Potatoes really have eyes.

TRUE. But not eyes like yours! Potato eyes are tiny buds, which grow into new potato plants.

Which plants live in fresh water?

Freshwater plants grow in ponds, lakes, rivers and streams. Most have roots which anchor them in mud at the bottom. Their stems grow through the water and their leaves and flowers open above the water's surface.

Water hyacinth

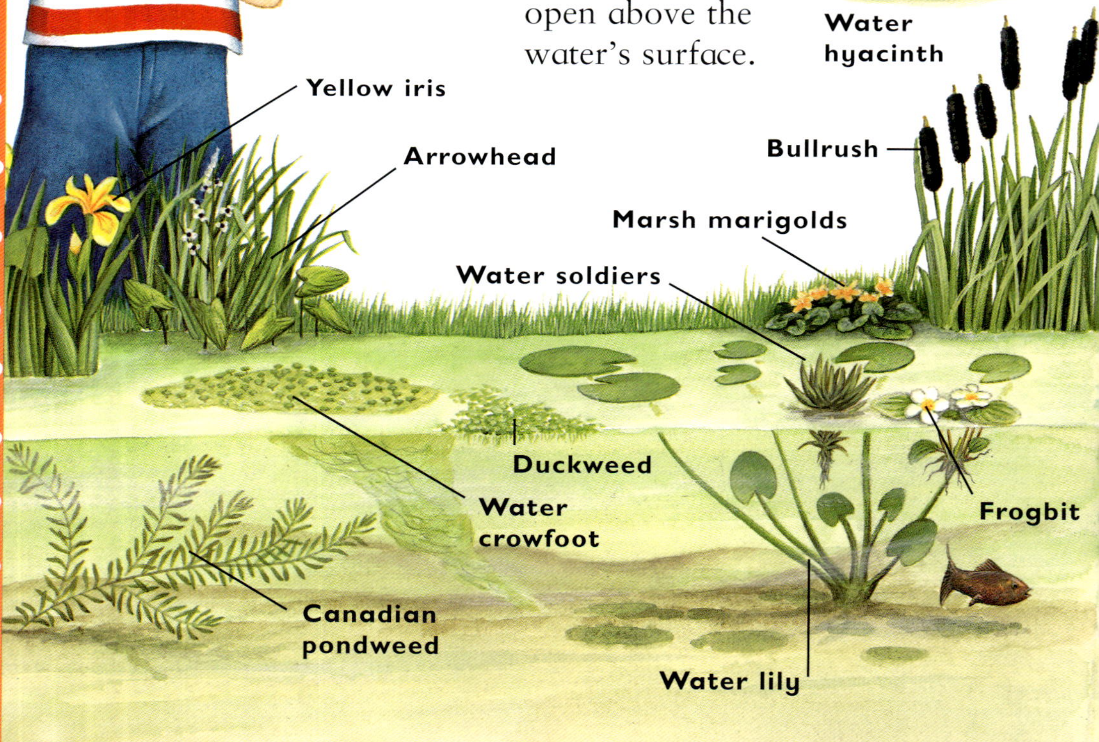

Which plants live in sea water?

Seaweeds do not have roots. Instead they fasten on to rocks using a structure called a holdfast.

Seaweed is a kind of plant called alga that lives in salty water. Algae can be red, brown, green or blue but they still contain chlorophyll for making food from sunlight. Some seaweeds fasten themselves on to rocks. Others have bubbles of air in their leaves so they can float.

True or False?

Water plants often have two kinds of leaves.

TRUE. Leaves below the water are often small to avoid water damage. Leaves above are larger, to catch the light.

Seaweed can grow as tall as trees.

TRUE. Kelp can grow up to 200 metres long! Forests of kelp grow near California.

Are some plants dangerous?

Some plants are poisonous to stop animals eating them. Poisonous plants include foxgloves, lupins, deadly nightshade and belladonna. Poison ivy may leave blisters if it touches bare skin. Nettles have tiny hairs on their leaves that inject you with poison if you brush against them.

Which plants have weapons?

Brambles and roses have thorns, cacti have sharp spines and holly has spiky leaves, to stop animals eating them.

Which plants eat meat?

Some plants eat insects as well as making their own food. When an insect touches a delicate hair on the inside of the leaves of a Venus flytrap, the leaves snap shut, trapping the insect inside. Insects landing on the edge of the pitcher plant slip into a pool of liquid at the bottom and drown.

True or False?

Some poison can be good for us.

TRUE. In small doses, the poison contained in the foxglove plant can be used as medicine to help people who have weak hearts.

Potatoes are poisonous.

TRUE. But only the leaves. The tubers are fine to eat.

Which plants can we eat?

We can eat all sorts of plants. We eat the leaves, roots and stalks of vegetable plants and all kinds of fruits and nuts. Sugar, spices, cereals (such as wheat and barley) and even chocolate come from plants.

How do plants help us?

Plants give us lots of other things as well as food. Cotton cloth comes from the cotton plant and linen comes from a plant called flax. Plants are also used to make oil, beauty products and medicines.

Eucalyptus (cold cures)

Cotton (clothes)

Seaweed (photographic film)

Oil seed rape (machine oil)

Aloe vera (face creams)

Foxglove (heart medicine)

True or False?

Plants give us good ideas.

TRUE. The burdock plant has tiny hooked spines. It gave us the idea for Velcro fasteners on clothes, shoes and bags.

This book was really made from plants.

TRUE. Books are made from paper. Most paper comes from trees.

Are plants in danger?

Plants are in danger from forest fires, pollution from car exhaust fumes and smoking factory chimneys. Building new homes and roads is also dangerous for the places where many plants live and grow.

Why are jungles in danger?

Jungles are in danger of being destroyed forever because so many trees are being cut down for wood or to clear land for farming. When this happens, many kinds of plants and animals may die out.

Can I help to protect plants?

Yes – don't pick wild flowers, especially in nature reserves. Try to grow a tree in your garden or in a park, or sow your own wild garden from seeds.

True or False?

Trees grow again if they are cut down.

TRUE. But very slowly. It takes hundreds of years for a whole forest to regrow. More than 400 types of plant die out every year.

Plants harm other plants.

TRUE. The strangler fig winds around a tree as it grows, until eventually the tree dies.

Questions and Answers about

Wings and Wheels

WHAT IS A MUSCLE CAR?
and other questions about motor cars

WHICH TRUCKS CRUSH CARS? and other questions about trucks and diggers

WHAT IS A STUNT PLANE?
and other questions about flying machines

WHAT IS THE SHUTTLE USED FOR?
and other questions about spacecraft

What is a muscle car?

and other questions about motor cars

How did people travel before cars?

Before cars were invented, people often travelled in wheeled carriages, pulled by teams of horses. The journey was dusty, uncomfortable and usually quite slow.

Early steam car

Did cars run on steam?

Several early cars ran on steam power, just like steam trains. Steam engines were more powerful than petrol engines, but they were very heavy and it was hard work to keep them running.

What fuel do cars use?

For over 100 years, most cars have run on petrol. At first there were very few petrol stations, so most drivers carried cans of spare fuel with them. Cars with petrol engines run more quickly than cars with steam engines.

Early petrol station

True or False?

The first cars were very fast.

FALSE. In Britain, a person with a red flag had to walk in front of all cars, to warn other road-users to keep out of the way.

Early drivers used to cover their faces.

TRUE. The first cars were uncovered, and the roads were dusty, so drivers had to wrap up all over for protection.

What was the first car?

The first car to be sold was the three-wheeled Benz Patent Motorwagen, in 1887. It looked more like a chair on wheels than a car, and was so slow that it couldn't travel up hills!

Benz Patent Motorwagen

How were early cars steered?

Early cars didn't have steering wheels. Instead, drivers steered with a lever, or by turning handles on a small wheel at the end of a pole.

Who was Daimler?

Gottlieb Daimler was a German engineer, who built the first ever motorcycle in 1885. He also built one of the first four-wheeled petrol driven cars. Daimler's cars were very difficult to drive, but they worked much better than other early cars.

Daimler's first car

True or False?

Early cars often used to break down.

TRUE. Early cars were very unreliable (they often broke down). Some motorists spent more time fixing their cars than driving them!

Cars had to be wound up.

TRUE. You didn't start early cars with a key. Instead, you wound a starting handle at the front.

When was the first car race?

The first car race was in 1894, between Paris and Rouen in France – 13 cars took part. The fastest was a huge de Dion steam tractor, which travelled at less than 19 kph.

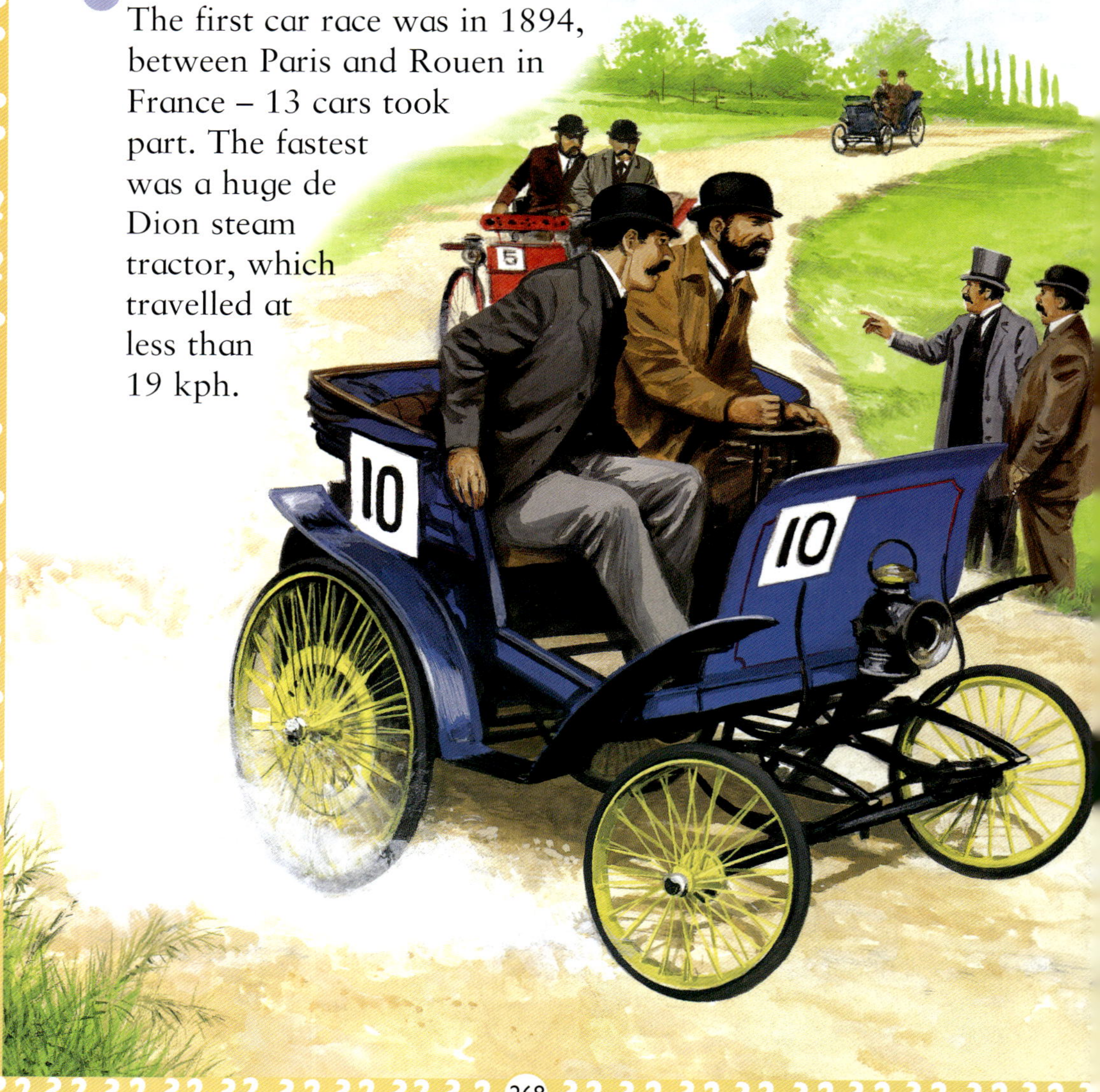

Early car race

What was a 'Blower Bentley'?

'Blower Bentleys' were very fast racing cars in the 1920s and 1930s. They were fitted with a blower, or supercharger, which drove extra fuel into the engine to make the car super-quick.

Blower Bentley

Which car was never happy?

Camille Jenatzy's electric car was called 'La Jamais Contente', ('never happy' in French). But Jenatzy was happy, when the car broke the world speed record.

'La Jamais Contente'

True or False?

Car races were dangerous.

TRUE. Early cars had very bad brakes, and often had accidents. Drivers weren't protected by helmets or seat belts, and races took place on public roads, crowded with spectators.

Rocket cars were invented long before space rockets.

TRUE. The Heylandt rocket car was first driven in 1931. The first space rocket flew 26 years later.

Austin Seven

Which car was a baby?

The Austin Seven was nicknamed the 'baby Austin' because it was so tiny. Four people could only just fit inside it, but it became Britain's most popular car in the 1920s.

Which cars only came in black?

The Model 'T' Ford, or 'Tin Lizzie', always left the factory painted black. In its day, the Model 'T' was the most popular car in the world. Over 15 million were built!

Model 'T' Ford

Charabanc

Which car travelled to the seaside?

Charabancs were the first motorised coaches. Groups of friends used to hire long charabancs for special trips to the seaside or to the city. The passengers sat on wooden benches behind the driver.

True or False?

Fords moved along a line.

TRUE. Fords were the first cars to be built on a moving line. Parts were added until the cars were finished at the end of the line.

All cars had hard roofs.

FALSE. Early cars had soft roofs which folded down. Motorists baked in the summer, and froze in the winter!

Which car was the most comfortable?

Rolls Royces are very quiet, comfortable and expensive cars. The 1907 Silver Ghost was no exception. Owners rarely drove themselves, but preferred to relax in the back!

Rolls Royce Silver Ghost

Which car was 'royal'?

Ettore Bugatti hoped that every royal family in Europe would buy a Bugatti Royale, but only six were ever built. Today, each one is worth millions of pounds.

Bugatti Royale

What was a Cord?

The Cord was one of the most comfortable American cars of the 1920s and 1930s, but they were very expensive, and very few were built. Luckily, many of them still exist.

Cord 810

True or False?

Passengers could eat a picnic in the car.

TRUE. Luxury cars, such as Rolls Royces, had picnic tables in the back, which folded down if passengers ever got peckish!

All cars had electric horns.

FALSE. Early motorists had to squeeze the horns on their cars, to warn other drivers. Horns on modern cars are powered by electricity.

Who built big family cars?

American cars were always much bigger than European cars. Their roads were wider, and petrol was also cheaper than in Europe, which meant that many American families could afford to run a large family car.

1939 Plymouth

What is a 'Beetle'?

The first Volkswagen was nicknamed the 'Beetle' or 'Bug' because it looks a bit like an insect. Over 40 million have been made since 1938.

Where was the first motorway?

Before cars were invented, most roads were narrow and bumpy. As cars became faster, bigger roads were needed. The first motorway was built in Germany in 1921.

Volkswagen Beetles

True or False?

Beetles are able to swim.

TRUE. During World War Two, the German army built a special Volkswagen Beetle, which could travel through rivers.

Motorists often lost their way.

TRUE. There used to be very few road signs, so it was difficult to find your way. Sensible motorists carried maps in their cars.

What is a rally car?

Rally cars are family cars, which have been given extra-powerful engines for off-road racing. Rally cars skid across country, through mud, snow and across ice. Accidents often happen, and drivers are protected by crash helmets and safety harnesses.

What is Formula One?

Formula One racing takes place around the world every year. Formula One cars have very powerful engines and huge fins, which stop the cars from taking off at high speed!

Formula One racing car

Rally car

How fast can racing cars go?

Formula One cars race at speeds of over 250 kph, but American Indycar racing is faster. Indycars can zoom along at 375 kph – that's over four times faster than the speed limit on American motorways.

Indycar racer

True or False?

All races are very short.

FALSE. Dragster races only last for a few seconds, but the Le Mans race in France lasts for 24 hours – a whole day and night!

Cars race through cities.

TRUE. Formula One races take place in cities in Monaco and Australia, but the streets are cleared of traffic and people before the race.

Which cars had fins?

During the 1950s, many colourful American cars, such as Oldsmobiles, had huge fins, shiny metal bumpers and bright lights fitted to them. Some of them looked more like alien spaceships than cars!

Which cars are stretched?

Limousines can be stretched, so that they are as long as a train. The longest limousine in the world had 26 wheels, a swimming pool, a bed and a helicopter landing pad! It was 30.5 m long – about ten times longer than a family car.

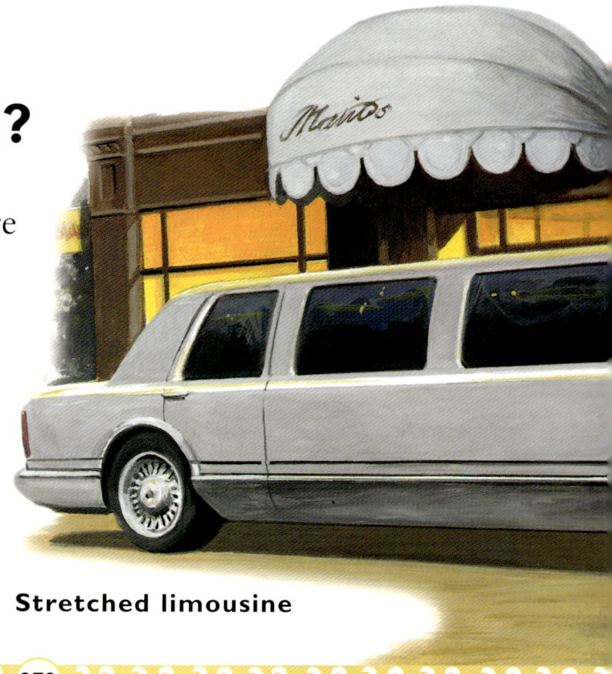

Stretched limousine

Tucker '48

Which car was a goose?

The Tucker '48 was an unusual car, nicknamed the 'Tin Goose'. The engine was at the back of the car, and its front headlight swivelled as the driver turned the steering wheel.

True or False?

Cars have at least four wheels.

FALSE. Some small cars, such as the Morgan three-wheeler and the Reliant Robin, only have three.

The gull wing looked like a sea gull.

TRUE. The doors on the 1952 Mercedes Benz 300 SL opened upwards. When they were fully open, the car looked a little like a sea gull, spreading its wings.

BMW Isetta 'bubble car'

Who travelled in a bubble?

The BMW Isetta was nicknamed the 'bubble car' because of its shape. These tiny three-wheelers only had one door, at the front. There was only room for the driver and one passenger.

Which car is smart?

The Smart Car is a very small modern car which is perfect for nipping around crowded cities. Because it's so short and slim, the Smart Car takes up very little room when it's not being used – drivers can park it sideways against the pavement.

Smart Car

Renault Zoom concept car

Which car can fold up?

The Renault Zoom can fold up its back wheels to make itself shorter, so that it can park in small spaces. It also has an electric motor, instead of a petrol engine, and doesn't make lots of dirty fumes like other cars.

True or False?

Frogeyes look like frogs.

TRUE. The Austin Healey Sprite was nicknamed the Frogeye, because its big headlights and radiator grille make it look like a cheeky, smiling frog!

You can race in a Mini.

TRUE. Minis won the Monte Carlo rally three times. They were good rally cars, partly because they could be steered around corners very quickly.

What is a sports car?

Ferrari F40

Sports cars are meant to be driven for fun. Often they have a fold-down roof, a small boot, and they're usually much faster than ordinary cars.

Which car is named after a snake?

AC Cobra

The AC Cobra is named after a poisonous snake. These cars have massive engines, fat tyres and extra-strong bodies for driving at high speed. Cobras make superb racing cars.

What is a muscle car?

Muscle cars are ordinary cars which have been souped-up for high performance. The Shelby Mustang was a Ford Mustang, specially tuned by racing driver Carroll Shelby.

Shelby Mustang

True or False?

Morgans are built by robots.

FALSE. Morgan sports cars are still built by hand. Early cars were always handmade, but modern cars are mostly built in large factories by robots.

All sports cars have engines at the front.

FALSE. Some sports cars, such as the Porsche 911, have their engine in the back, and their boot at the front of the car.

What was an Aerocar?

The Aerocar was a car which could really fly. When it was driving on the road, the Aerocar folded up its wings and tail.

Aerocar

Which car could dive underwater?

In the film The Spy Who Loved Me, James Bond's Lotus sports car could turn into a submarine and swim underwater. People got a shock when they saw it driving out of the water on to a beach!

James Bond's Lotus Esprit

What is a hot rod?

A hot rod is an old family car which has been given an extra-powerful engine, a lowered roof, huge tyres and a colourful paint job. Hot rods are raced all over the world.

Hot rods

True or False?

Some cars are funny.

TRUE. Funny cars are family cars with stretched bodies and huge engines which take part in dragster races.

All cars are made in factories.

FALSE. Some sports cars can be bought in kit form, to be built at home just like a model aeroplane, only much bigger!

What is a dragster?

A dragster is a very powerful racing car, which races along a short track at enormous speed. Dragsters are so fast that brakes alone can't stop them – they also need parachutes to slow them down.

Thrust SSC

Dragster

What's the fastest car ever?

Thrust SSC was the first car to travel faster than the speed of sound, in 1997. Thrust had four parachutes and two massive jet engines, which are normally used to power fighter aircraft!

Which bird travelled at 484 kph?

Malcolm Campbell broke the land speed record nine times in his Bluebird cars during the 1930s. 484 kph is about twice as fast as a modern sports car can travel.

Bluebird

True or False?

The McLaren F1 can reach 384 kph.

TRUE. Only a few McLaren F1s were ever built, but their lucky owners got to drive the fastest road car ever built. It was also one of the most expensive!

Rocket cars are faster than jet cars.

FALSE. The rocket-powered Blue Flame reached over 1,000 kph in 1970. But jet-powered Thrust SSC was over 200 kph faster.

Which car could drive itself?

KITT was the name of a special car in the television series Knightrider. KITT could drive on its own, and could even talk to its owner, to warn him if he was being followed by baddies!

KITT

What was Chitty Chitty Bang Bang?

Only three Chitty Chitty Bang Bang cars were built. They had huge, powerful plane engines, and won many races, even though they were difficult to drive and hardly had any brakes.

Chitty Chitty Bang Bang

Which car had an ejector seat?

James Bond's Aston Martin DB5 had an ejector seat. When he wanted to get rid of someone, Bond pressed a button, the roof opened, and his passenger was shot into the air!

Aston Martin DB5

True or False?

Some cars are bulletproof.

TRUE. Many important people travel in bulletproof cars made of tough metal and glass. Bulletproof cars are very heavy and expensive.

Queen Elizabeth doesn't have number plates.

TRUE. The Queen is the only person in Britain without number plates on her car. Plates tell the police where a car comes from and who owns it.

What was Sunraycer?

Every year, there's a race in Australia for cars which use sunshine for fuel. Sunraycer was an unusual-looking car which crossed the country at a speed of about 40 kph. Luckily, there's plenty of sunshine in Australia!

Sunraycer

Which car fits in a suitcase?

This strange Japanese compact car is so small, that it can fit into a suitcase. At the end of the journey, the case folds up, and the driver can carry the car away.

How fast can electric cars travel?

Electric cars are usually slower than petrol-driven cars, but one electric three-wheeler called Alien was said to have reached 240 kph – as fast as a modern sports car.

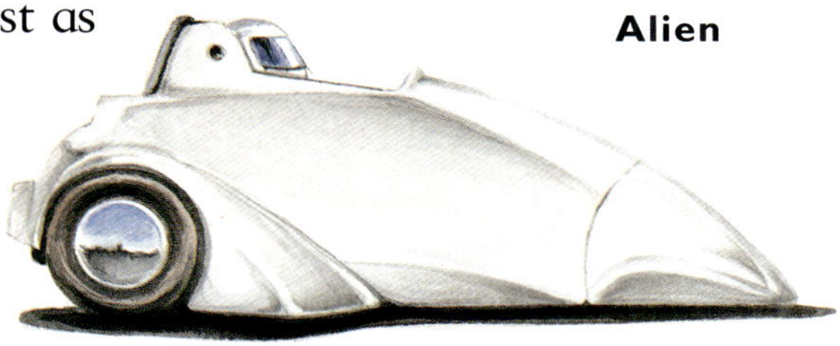

Alien

True or False?

Some cars have sails.

TRUE. Sand yachts are sailing boats on wheels. The wind in their sails can push these three-wheelers to 125 kph.

Some electric cars use petrol.

TRUE. Combination cars are electric cars with a petrol generator. The generator charges the electric batteries, which give power to the car.

Which trucks crush cars?

and other questions about trucks and diggers

Dray-horses and cart

Were there trucks before engines?

Before engines were invented, heavy loads were pulled on carts by teams of large dray-horses. Strong dray-horses were also used to pull ploughs on farms before motorised tractors were invented.

Steam truck

Which coach ran on steam?

Dr Church's steam coach was built in England in 1833. Up to 50 passengers rode on it, on long journeys between cities. It must have been very noisy and uncomfortable.

Dr Church's steam coach

What did steam trucks look like?

Steam trucks looked like steam trains, with large engines, big iron wheels and smoky funnels. They were so big and heavy that they ruined the roads.

True or False?

Early trucks were huge.

FALSE. Steam trucks were the largest vehicles on the road, but they were still much smaller than modern trucks.

Steam trucks were very slow.

TRUE. In England, someone had to walk in front of the first trucks, with a red flag to warn other road-users.

Which car was a truck?

Many early trucks were really cars which had been given extra parts and made stronger, to carry heavy loads. This 1919 truck was based on the popular Model 'T' Ford car.

Model 'T' Ford truck

What does 'cab-over-engine' mean?

A cab-over-engine truck is a truck where the driver's cab is on top of the engine. When the engine needs to be repaired, the whole cab tips forward to give the mechanic a good look.

What replaced steam trucks?

Steam trucks were noisy, dirty and not very reliable. Petrol-powered trucks first appeared in 1896, and were much more popular. These days, most trucks run on diesel fuel.

Dennis

True or False?

Some trucks had no tyres.

TRUE. Before air-filled tyres were invented, trucks had huge, heavy wheels made of metal.

Anyone can drive a truck.

FALSE. It's more difficult to drive a truck than an ordinary car. Truck drivers have to pass a test before they're allowed to drive a truck on the road.

Which trucks bend in the middle?

Long articulated trucks, which pull separate trailers, bend in the middle – if they didn't, they wouldn't be able to turn round sharp corners. Shorter trucks, which are built in one piece and don't bend in the middle, are called rigid trucks.

Articulated truck

Which trucks have piggybacks?

New trucks are sometimes delivered by being towed behind another truck, like a trailer. This means that there's less wear on the new trucks' tyres, less fuel is burned and only one driver is needed to move several trucks.

Which trucks deliver cars?

Transporters can deliver up to ten cars at a time. The cars are driven on to the transporter up ramps, and they're very carefully strapped down during the journey, so they don't roll off!

Transporter

Piggyback trucks

True or False?

Trucks sneeze.

TRUE. Have you ever noticed how trucks make a hissing noise, like a sneeze? That's the sound of air escaping from their brakes.

Truckers set their trucks on fire.

FALSE. But drivers in very cold countries do make fires under their trucks, to stop the diesel fuel from freezing.

Low-loader

What is a low-loader?

A low-loader is a large transporter truck with a low trailer at the rear. Other vehicles, such as cars, tractors and even tanks, are driven up its ramps and on to the trailer.

Half-track army truck

Which trucks can travel through water?

Special army trucks, called amphibious trucks, can travel on land and through shallow rivers. The underside of the truck is tightly sealed so that water can't flood into the cab or into the engine.

Amphibious truck

What are caterpillar tracks?

Caterpillar tracks are knobbly strips of metal or rubber, which wrap around the wheels of tanks, bulldozers and other off-road vehicles. They stop the wheels from getting stuck in muddy or sandy ground.

True or False?

Some trucks wear armour.

TRUE. Some army trucks are covered in very strong metal armour-plating to protect them.

Tanks had caterpillar tracks first.

FALSE. Caterpillar tracks were first used to stop tractors getting stuck in muddy fields. Soldiers guessed they would work just as well on tanks.

Air-lines

How do trucks stop?

Trucks use air-brakes to stop. An air compressor in the truck sucks in air and squashes it. When the driver presses the brake pedal, the squashed air travels along coiled air-lines and pushes brake shoes against the wheels, slowing them down.

What is a jack-knife?

A jack-knife is a dangerous accident where a truck slows down, but its trailer slides sideways out of control, sometimes spilling its load on to the road. A jack-knife is named after a knife with a folding blade.

This transporter has jack-knifed.

Why do trucks have so many gears?

Trucks sometimes have over 15 gears, compared to only five or six in a car. Heavy trucks need plenty of low gears to go up and down steep hills, and higher gears to cruise along the open road.

True or False?

Trucks aren't able to climb steep hills.

FALSE. Trucks can climb hills, but because they're much heavier than cars, they can't do it very fast!

Truckers need to rest.

TRUE. Truck drivers have to take regular breaks in case they get sleepy at the wheel and cause an accident.

What is a customised truck?

Truckers often want their trucks to look different from everyone else's. They can customise their trucks by painting them with bright patterns and colours, or by adding extra lights or shiny metal bodywork.

Customised truck

Tractor tugger

What are tractor tuggers?

Tractor tuggers are powered by fiery aircraft engines! They have to pull a load of 100 tonnes (as heavy as 100 family cars) for 100 m in special competitions.

Which trucks crush cars?

Monster trucks are small pickup trucks, which have been fitted with enormous dumper-truck wheels. They take part in races, and drive over large obstacles, including cars, crushing them as flat as pancakes!

Monster truck

True or False?

Some trucks can jump.

TRUE. Stunt drivers drive their trucks very quickly up ramps, and fly over rows of cars and other obstacles.

Trucks can do wheelies.

TRUE. By revving the engine very hard, stunt drivers can lift the front wheels of their trucks into the air. That's called doing a wheelie.

What is a road train?

A road train is a very strong truck, which pulls not one, but several long trailers. Road trains make very long journeys in big countries, such as Australia.

Road train

Which is the biggest truck?

The biggest truck in the world is a dumper truck called the Terex Titan. Each of its wheels is twice as high as a person, and weighs as much as three family cars!

Terex Titan

What is a digger?

A digger digs earth out of the ground with a large bucket on the end of a moving arm. Most diggers move around on caterpillar tracks.

Digger

True or False?

Terex Titan travels on the road.

FALSE. Terex Titan is too big to travel on the road. Instead it's taken to pieces, and each part is carried on a transporter.

Some trucks need help from the police.

TRUE. Trucks pulling very large loads need the police to travel with them, to warn other drivers to get out of the way.

Where do truckers sleep?

Truckers are often on the road for several days at a time, and need somewhere to sleep away from home. Some truckers sleep in their cabs, in a bed behind the seats.

Where do truckers eat?

There are truck stops on main roads all over the world, where truckers can get a bite to eat, fill up with fuel, wash their clothes, and sometimes even have their hair cut!

How do truckers talk to each other?

Truckers talk to each other on the move using citizens' band (C.B.) radio. Every trucker has a nickname, and can warn other drivers of hazards, such as traffic jams or bad weather.

Truck stop

True or False?

Trucks are scrubbed clean.

TRUE. Most truck stops have a drive-through truck wash, where trucks are scrubbed clean with huge soapy brushes.

Trucks never break down.

FALSE. Trucks do break down sometimes. There are usually teams of mechanics and plenty of spare parts at truck stops.

Forklift trucks

Which small trucks carry heavy loads?

Forklift trucks can carry heavy loads around factories, on wooden platforms called pallets. The driver slides the forks underneath the pallets, lifts them into the air, and moves them to another part of the factory.

Which trucks carry logs?

Loggers are large trucks, which carry logs from forests to factories. Logs are much too heavy to be put on a truck by hand, so a logger has its own crane that picks up the logs and puts them on the back of the truck.

Logger

Do trucks pull aeroplanes?

Airport tugs are strong enough to pull large aeroplanes. These short trucks fit under an aeroplane's nose, and fix on to its front wheel.

Airport tug

True or False?

All trucks have one engine.

FALSE. Some trucks pull such heavy loads that one engine isn't enough. Terex Titan is so huge, it needs an engine for each wheel!

Trucks can lift cars.

TRUE. In many cities, the police drive special trucks, which can lift up and take away illegally parked cars.

Freezer truck

Which trucks are freezing?

A freezer truck is like a big fridge on wheels. It's used to transport food, such as ice cream, which has to stay cold in case it melts.

How is petrol delivered?

Petrol is delivered to petrol stations in tankers. A tanker can carry enough petrol to fill up about 500 family cars. The petrol is pumped into a large tank, buried beneath the station.

Petrol tanker

Container truck

What is a container truck?

Many of the goods you see in the shops are made overseas, and arrive on ships in metal boxes called containers. The containers are lifted off the ships and put on to large container trucks, which drive them straight to the shops.

True or False?

Some trucks tip up.

TRUE. A tipper truck has a special lifting body, which tips up, so that its load simply slides out of the back.

You can fly in a truck.

FALSE. But cherry pickers lift people into the air on a long arm, to do jobs such as changing bulbs in street lamps.

Garbage truck

Which truck eats rubbish?

Garbage trucks eat rubbish. A special device crushes the rubbish to make it smaller, and the truck gobbles it up, before being emptied at the dump, ready for the next journey.

Wrecker

What is a wrecker?

'Wrecker' is the name for a large North American breakdown truck, which can tow away other trucks or cars, if they've broken down or had an accident.

Which trucks mix cement?

Cement and other ingredients are mixed together in a cement mixer, to make concrete, which is used to make buildings. The ingredients are put in the mixer's drum, which spins around. When the concrete is ready, it's poured out of the cement mixer.

Cement mixer

True or False?

Garbage trucks pick up rubbish.

TRUE. Some garbage trucks can pick up dustbins with mechanical arms, shake them until they're empty, then put them down again.

Trucks have to be weighed.

TRUE. When trucks pass from one country or state into another, they often have to be weighed, to work out how much tax they need to pay.

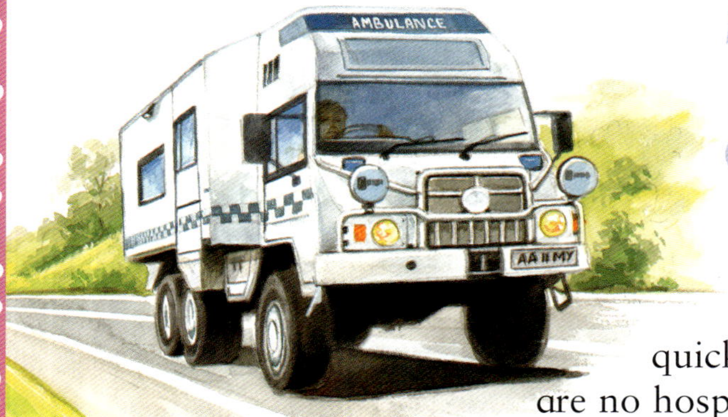

Mobile hospital

Which trucks are hospitals?

An ambulance is a small truck full of emergency equipment, which takes ill people to hospital quickly. But in areas where there are no hospitals, doctors and nurses treat patients in larger trucks called mobile hospitals, where they can even perform life-saving operations.

Which truck puts out fires?

Fire trucks are packed full of equipment to put out fires. They have powerful hoses, medical equipment, axes for breaking down doors, and ladders to reach fires in tall buildings.

Fire truck

Security van

Which trucks are safe?

Armour-plated security vans collect money from shops and banks. It's important that the money isn't stolen, so it's kept in a safe, which even the van driver can't open.

True or False?

All fire trucks have one driver.

FALSE. Fire trucks with very long ladders, have a second driver who sits on the ladder, steering it safely around corners.

Some fire trucks squirt foam.

TRUE. It's very dangerous to squirt water at fires caused by electricity. Firefighters put out electrical fires with foam instead.

Paris-Dakar back-up truck

Which trucks travel through the desert?

The Paris-Dakar rally is a very long race for cars and motorbikes through the dusty Sahara desert. Back-up trucks come along too, full of spare parts, in case any of the racers crashes or breaks down.

Are there truck races?

You can race almost anything on wheels, including trucks. There are bumpy cross-country rallies, and races around tracks. Some racing trucks are even powered by huge jet engines, and can whizz along more quickly than an express train!

Pickup racer

Can you race a pickup?

Pickup trucks are small trucks, which are normally used for carrying small loads, but they can also be raced. Souped-up versions, with low bodies, streamlined shapes and extra-powerful engines race around circuits in America.

Racing trucks

True or False?

A pickup is the fastest truck.

FALSE. The Hawaiian Fire Department's customised fire truck is the fastest ever truck. It has a top speed of over 650 kph!

Some trucks are dragsters.

TRUE. Pairs of dragster trucks, with massive engines and huge rear tyres, race each other at high speed along a very short track.

Bulldozer

What is a bulldozer?

A bulldozer is a heavy vehicle used on building sites. It runs on caterpillar tracks, and has a large blade at the front, for moving or flattening the ground. Bulldozers are also powerful enough to knock down old buildings.

Backhoe loader

Which digger does lots of jobs?

A backhoe loader can dig, drill and pick things up. Different parts fix on to its rear arm for breaking up concrete, making holes in the ground or scooping up soil. It also has a shovel at the front for picking up earth and rubble.

What is a mobile crane?

A mobile crane is part truck and part crane. It can be driven on to building sites, where the driver operates the crane from a cab at the back, lifting heavy loads of concrete or metal.

Mobile crane

True or False?

Diggers have corkscrews.

TRUE. Backhoe loaders often have corkscrew-shaped drills, but they're used for boring holes, not for opening bottles!

Some diggers have hammers.

TRUE. Some diggers have powerful, noisy hammers, called pile drivers, that bang large fence-posts into the ground.

What is a stunt plane?

and other questions about flying machines

Who flew the first kites?

The Chinese used to fly kites hundreds of years ago to see if there was enough wind for them to set sail in their ships.

Montgolfière balloon

Who was the first person to fly?

François Pilâtre de Rozier and the Marquis d'Arlandes flew a Montgolfière balloon in 1783. They travelled 8 km over Paris, at a height of 900 m.

What are gliders?

Gliders are flying machines without engines. Otto Lilienthal built lots of gliders over 100 years ago. He used to fly them by hanging from a bar under the wings. Sadly, he was killed in a glider crash in 1896.

Otto Lilienthal

True or False?

People flew with strap-on wings.

FALSE. 'Bird-men' did try to fly by flapping strap-on wings, but no one ever succeeded.

Balloons can fly all around the world.

TRUE. The Breitling Orbiter made the first round-the-world balloon flight in 1999. The journey took nearly three weeks!

Which plane ran on steam power?

The odd-looking Eole was flown a short way by Clément Ader in 1890. This steam-powered plane only managed to fly about 20 cm above the ground.

Eole

Who were the Wright brothers?

Wilbur and Orville Wright were American bicycle makers, who built the first successful aeroplane with an engine. Orville flew the Flyer for twelve seconds in 1903.

Flyer

What is a biplane?

A biplane is a small aeroplane, such as the Sopwith Camel, with two pairs of wings, one above the other. Most early planes were biplanes, and they are still used today for stunt flying.

Sopwith Camel

True or False?

One plane had 20 wings.

TRUE. Horatio Phillips thought that his Multiplane would fly better if it had 20 small wings. He was wrong, and it only made a few short hops in 1907.

Early planes were very fast.

FALSE. Early racing cars were much faster than aeroplanes, but by 1920 flying was the quickest way to travel.

What was a Zeppelin?

A Zeppelin was a type of airship which flew during the early 20th century. It was filled with hydrogen gas and the passengers travelled in a very comfortable area under the main body of the airship.

Giffard's airship

Who flew in a steam-powered airship?

In 1852, Henri Giffard flew the very first airship, which had a small steam engine and a propeller. It was a slow journey. His airship could only travel at 8 kph.

Modern airship

Graf Zeppelin

Do people still fly airships?

People still fly airships in many parts of the world, but they don't usually carry passengers these days. Airships often carry television cameras to film sporting events from the sky.

True or False?

Airships are very large.

TRUE. The largest airships were over twice as long as a football pitch, and much larger than the biggest aeroplanes.

Airships can only make short journeys.

FALSE. Airships used to fly all the way from Europe to America. The journey took about two days.

What was a Blériot?

Blériot XI

Louis Blériot made aeroplanes and also flew them. In 1909, he became the very first person to fly across the English Channel, when he flew his own Blériot XI plane from France to England.

Who were the first to fly across the Atlantic Ocean?

The first non-stop flight across the Atlantic was by John Alcock and Arthur Brown in 1919. Their Vickers Vimy plane crash-landed at the end of the flight, but luckily they escaped unhurt.

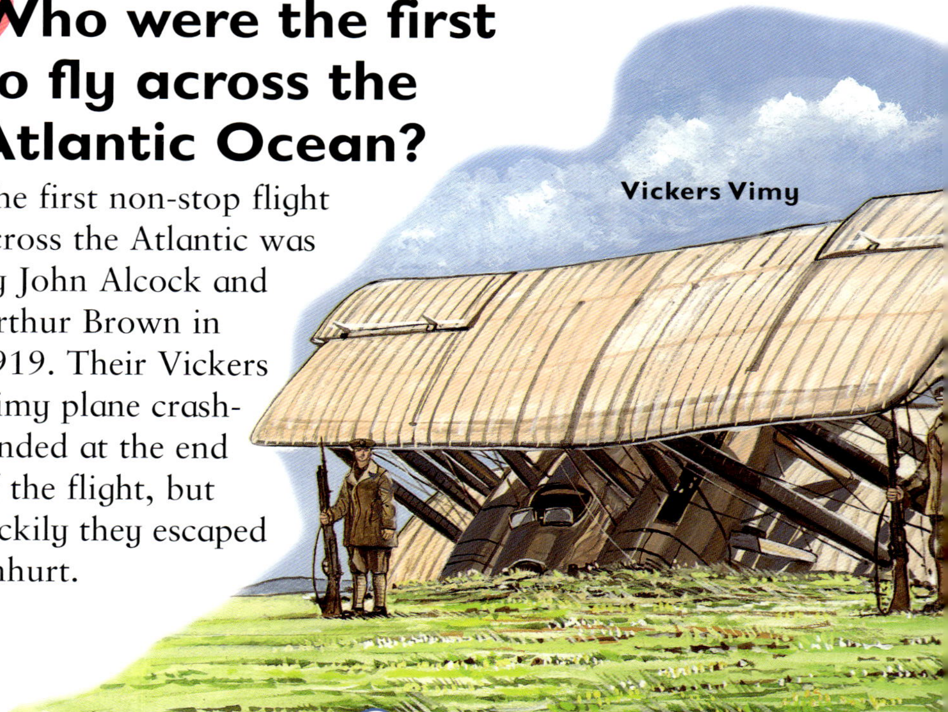

Vickers Vimy

Who were the first to fly across the Pacific Ocean?

Charles Kingsford Smith, Charles Ulm and their crew made the first flight across the Pacific in 1928, in their plane Southern Cross. They nearly crashed the plane into some trees when they landed on a small island during the journey.

True or False?

You can fly on a moth.

TRUE. Amy Johnson was the first person to fly alone from England to Australia in a biplane called a Gypsy Moth.

Lindbergh fell asleep at the controls.

TRUE. Charles Lindbergh took over 33 hours to fly across the Atlantic Ocean. No wonder he nodded off a few times!

Supermarine S 6B seaplane

Which planes have floats?

Seaplanes have floats instead of wheels, so that they can take off and land on water, using the sea as a runway.

What is a flying boat?

A flying boat is an aeroplane which has a body shaped like a large boat. Its wings are attached to the top of the plane, so that it can take off and land safely on water.

Which planes can only fly very low?

Surface-effect vehicles are special planes which only fly a few metres above the surface of the water. Their tiny wings won't allow them to rise high into the air.

Surface-effect vehicle

Canopus flying boat

True or False?

The Spruce Goose only flew once.

TRUE. Spruce Goose was so huge it could have held 700 passengers! It only flew once in 1947, and is now in a museum.

Some planes can give piggybacks.

TRUE. Flying boats are often so big that they are able to give piggybacks to smaller planes, including seaplanes.

Who flew a Meteor?

The Gloster Meteor was the first working British warplane with jet engines. It first flew in 1944, and was much faster than planes with propellers.

Who cut through the air with a Sabre?

The F-86 Sabre was an American jet fighter which first flew after World War Two. The Sabre was very fast and popular with the lucky pilots who were chosen to fly it.

de Havilland Comet

What was a Comet?

The de Havilland Comet was the first jet airliner to carry passengers. It had four jet engines set into its wings, and started flying between England and South Africa in 1952.

F-86 Sabre

True or False?

All jet planes fly very quickly.

FALSE. The Fairchild Republic A-10 can only fly very slowly, but it can turn and climb really quickly.

One plane had eight jet engines.

TRUE. The Boeing B-52 Stratofortress was so big, and flew so far, that it needed eight jet engines to keep it in the air!

Chuck Yeager

Who first flew faster than sound?

American test pilot Chuck Yeager was the first person to fly faster than sound in 1947. He flew a rocket-powered Bell X-1, which he nicknamed Glamorous Glennis after his wife.

Which plane is a Blackbird?

The American Lockheed Blackbird plane is the fastest jet plane of all time. In 1974, it flew from America to England in less than two hours!

X-15 rocket plane

What is a rocket plane?

Rocket planes have powerful rocket engines, which make them even faster than jet planes. The X-15 rocket plane is the fastest plane ever. It has also flown the highest – nearly 108 kilometres above the ground.

Blackbird

True or False?

Some planes are invisible to radar.

TRUE. The American 'Stealth' plane has flat surfaces and special paint, which make it very difficult for radar systems to see.

Jet planes can fly in space.

FALSE. Jet engines need air to work, and there's no air in space. Only rocket engines work in space.

What is a delta wing?

Most planes have slim and straight wings, but some very fast planes, such as the Saab Draken and Concorde, have much larger delta wings, which are shaped like a triangle, and help the plane to travel through the air quickly.

Saab J 35F Draken

Which plane had no wings?

The X-24B had no wings. Instead, this rocket plane had a specially shaped body which helped lift the plane and keep it in the air. Only very skilled pilots could fly wingless planes.

Which plane has back-to-front wings?

The Grumman X-29A has wings which face forwards, so that the plane can turn sharp corners when it's travelling very quickly. The plane is difficult to control, and it can only be flown with the help of computers.

Grumman X-29A

True or False?

Some planes can swing their wings.

TRUE. The Panavia Tornado swings its wings forwards to take off and land, and swings them back to fly at high speeds.

Triplanes have two wings.

FALSE. Triplanes have three sets of wings. The most famous triplane was the Red Baron's Dr I, flown in World War One.

What is a stunt plane?

Stunt planes are usually small, agile aircraft, flown by very brave and skilful pilots. They thrill crowds by flying in groups, performing stunts, such as loops and rolls, and flying very close to the ground.

Gee Bee racing planes

Are there plane races?

There have been plane races almost since planes were invented. The most famous racers were the Gee Bees. These short, fat planes flew in America during the 1930s in races that were 8,000 km long.

Where can I see stunt planes?

Air shows take place all over the world, where you can see planes of all shapes and sizes, including stunt display teams. Why not find out if there's an air show near you?

Stunt planes

True or False?

Planes can't fly upside down.

FALSE. Stunt planes often fly upside down. But pilots have to make sure that they're safely strapped in, to stop them falling out!

People can stand on planes' wings.

TRUE. 'Wing walkers' have to be tightly strapped on to the wing, and wrapped up in several layers of warm clothing!

Boeing 747 'Jumbo Jet'

How far can airliners travel?

Airliners can fly to the other side of the world in about 22 hours. They have to stop to fill up with fuel during the journey.

Concorde

What is the fastest airliner?

The fastest ever airliner is Concorde, which can travel at over twice the speed of sound. Concorde has made the trip between Europe and America in under three hours.

Can planes land in cities?

Small, quiet planes, such as the Dash-7, only need a short runway to take off and land. They are the ideal aircraft for small airports in crowded cities.

Dash-7

True or False?

Planes can fly themselves.

TRUE. Modern airliners have 'automatic pilot' computers which can fly the plane. So, don't worry if you see the pilot going for a walk during a flight!

Concorde is the biggest airliner.

FALSE. Concorde is the fastest airliner, but the Boeing 747 'Jumbo Jet' is the biggest airliner of all.

Westland Sea King

Which type of aircraft hovers?

Unlike aircraft with fixed wings, helicopters have wings called rotors, which spin around very quickly to lift them off the ground. Helicopters can also hover (stay still in the air without moving forwards or backwards).

What is an air ambulance?

Helicopters are often used as ambulances. They can land easily in cities, on roads or in parks, and they can take sick or injured people to hospital more quickly than a road ambulance.

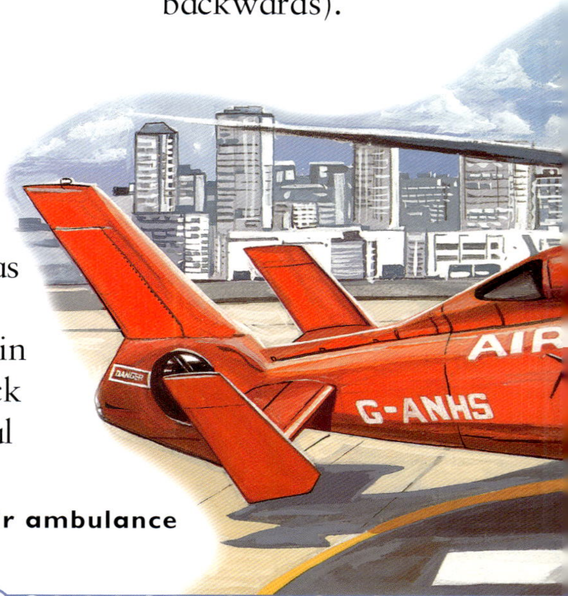

Air ambulance

X-wing plane

Which plane is also a helicopter?

The X-wing plane is half aeroplane, half helicopter. It takes off using its rotors, but once the X-wing is in the air, its blades stop spinning, and it moves forwards using two powerful jet engines.

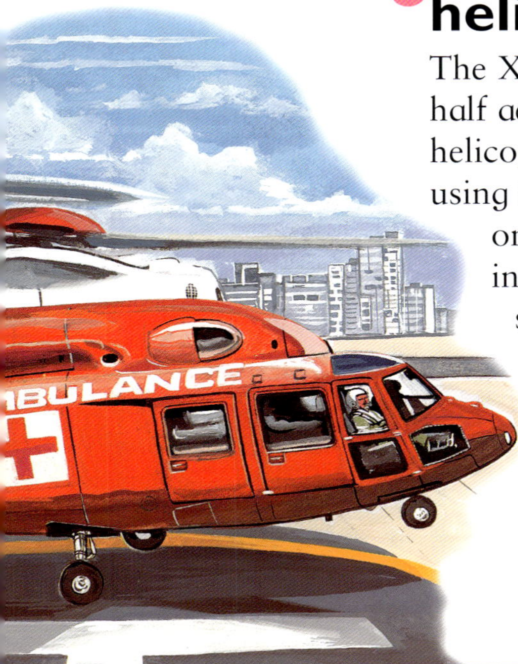

True or False?

All helicopters are very small.

FALSE. The huge Chinook helicopter can carry as many as 44 passengers – much more than many aeroplanes.

Helicopters can be used for sea rescue.

TRUE. Because they can hover, helicopters are very useful for rescuing people stranded at sea.

Bell rocket belt

What is a rocket belt?

The Bell rocket belt is a small aircraft, which straps on to its pilot. By working the rocket engines, the pilot can take off and hover, but the belt can only fly for about 30 seconds.

What is a jump-jet?

Some aircraft, such as the Harrier jump-jet, can take off straight up into the air without the need for a runway. They can also hover in the air.

Harrier jump-jet

Osprey

Which plane can swivel its engines?

The Osprey can swivel its propeller-driven engines, so that it can take off like a helicopter. Then the engines tilt forwards, and it flies like an ordinary plane.

True or False?

You can fly on a bed.

FALSE. But one early plane, which could take off like a jump-jet, looked so much like a bed that it was nicknamed the Flying Bedstead.

Planes have ejector seats.

TRUE. If they are in danger, the pilots of some military planes can press a button and shoot straight out of the cockpit!

What is a microlight?

Microlights are tiny aircraft powered by a small engine. The pilot sits in an open cockpit under the wing, and steers the plane by moving the wing.

Microlight

Hang-glider

What is a hang-glider?

A hang-glider is a very light aircraft with no engine. The pilot hangs in a harness under the wing, and steers the hang-glider with a control bar.

Paraglider

What is a paraglider?

Paragliders look like parachutes. Sometimes pilots have a strap-on engine, or they're towed behind speed boats. As it moves along, the paraglider fills with air, and lifts its pilot up into the sky.

True or False?

You can dive in the sky.

TRUE. Skydivers jump from planes high in the sky. They only open their parachutes as they get close to the ground.

Planes are always made in factories.

FALSE. Microlights often come in kit form. You can build them at home.

What will airliners look like in the future?

There are plans to build new super-jumbo jets, with over 600 seats. These triple-decker planes might solve the problem of the skies becoming overcrowded with air traffic.

Which plane travels in space?

The space shuttle is launched using huge rockets, which fall away as it reaches space. It has rocket engines of its own, to steer, speed up and slow down in space.

Which airliner might go into space?

One day, space planes might be able to fly passengers far above the Earth at amazing speeds. A trip between Europe and America in a space plane would only take half an hour!

True or False?

The shuttle is a glider.

TRUE. The space shuttle's engines run out of fuel in space. When the shuttle returns to Earth, it floats down as a glider.

The shuttle is covered in tiles.

TRUE. The shuttle gets very hot when it returns to Earth. It has thousands of special tiles which protect it from the heat.

What is the shuttle used for?

and other questions about spacecraft

Who invented the first rockets?

Small firework-like rockets were invented in China about 1,000 years ago. The Chinese used to fire them at their enemies during battles.

Which rocket first used liquid fuel?

Robert Goddard launched the first liquid-fuelled rocket in 1926. His rocket only went 12.5 m into the air (about as high as seven tall people), and landed 64 m away. All spacecraft are launched using liquid fuel rockets.

Why do spacecraft need rockets?

Jet engines and petrol engines need air to work. They would be no use in space, because there's no air in space. Rocket engines don't need air, so they can work just as well in space as they do on Earth.

Ariane rocket

True or False?

Spacecraft can be fired out of guns.

FALSE. Early scientists tried to launch spacecraft from guns, but they all crashed back down to Earth.

Early rockets went to space.

FALSE. Early rockets were mostly used as weapons during wartime. It wasn't until 1957 that a rocket travelled to space.

Sputnik 1

What is a satellite?

A satellite is any object which orbits (travels round and round) the Earth. The Earth's natural satellite is the Moon. The first man-made satellite was Sputnik 1, which was launched in 1957.

How do satellites use the Sun?

Satellites can carry on working for a long time because the Sun gives them energy. Satellites have solar panels, like wings, which soak up light and heat from the Sun, and turn them into electricity.

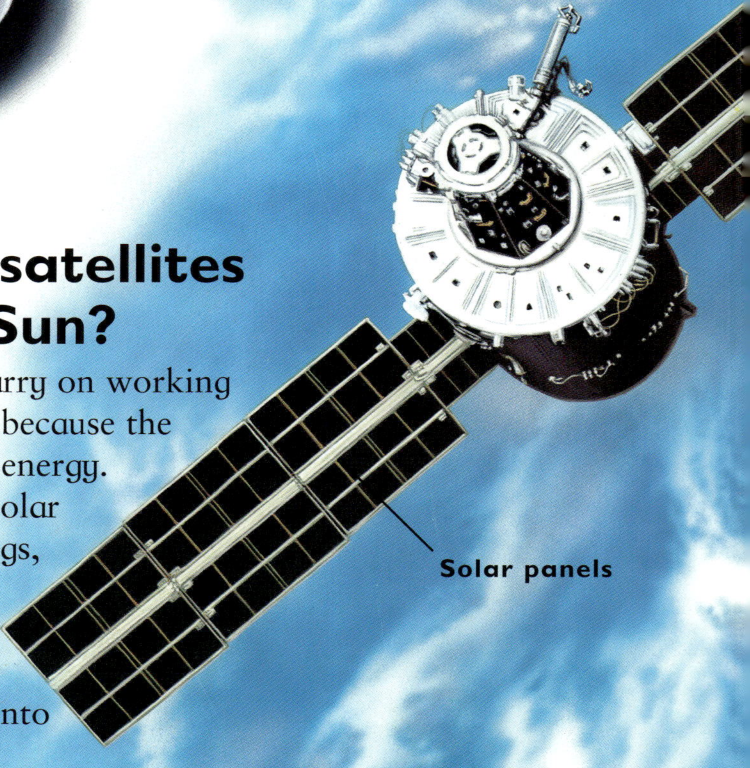
Solar panels

What do satellites do?

Satellites do lots of jobs. Some of them take pictures of Earth to tell us about the weather, and some are used for spying on other countries. Communications satellites bounce television and telephone signals back to Earth.

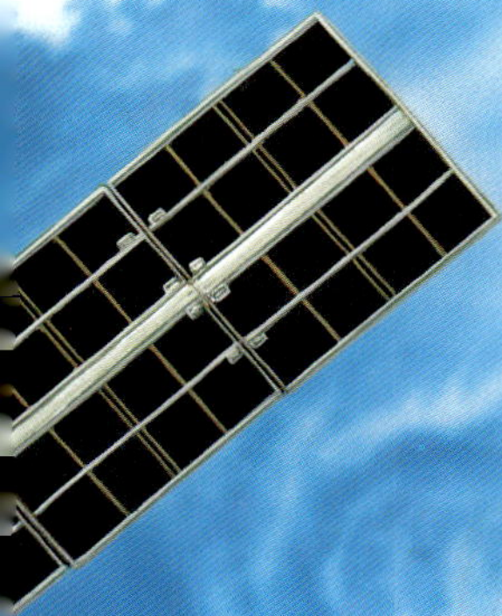

Telstar communications satellite

True or False?

Outer space is very windy.

FALSE. There is no air or wind in space. The flag on the Moon had to be held up with a wire, so that it looked as if it was blowing in the wind.

Outer space is freezing cold.

TRUE. Outer space is very cold indeed, unless the Sun's shining on you, when it's extremely hot.

Who was the first astronaut?

The first earthling in space wasn't a person – it was a Russian dog called Laika. She spent seven days orbiting the Earth aboard a small spacecraft called Sputnik 2 in 1957. Laika's journey proved that space flight would be safe for humans.

Laika

Yuri Gagarin

Who was the first person in space?

Russian pilot Yuri Gagarin became the first person in space in 1961. He orbited the Earth once in a Vostok 1 spacecraft. His journey only took an hour and a half. He was given a hero's welcome when he returned to Earth.

Who went back to space after 36 years?

John Glenn became the first American to orbit the Earth in 1962, when he was 41 years old. 36 years later, he went back, and became the oldest ever astronaut. He carried out experiments to see if space travel was more dangerous for older people.

True or False?

Laika was the only animal in space.

FALSE. Spiders, bees, shrimps, chimpanzees, tortoises, frogs, goldfish and jellyfish have all been to space.

You can walk in space.

TRUE. The first space-walk was by a Russian astronaut in 1965. He was roped to his spacecraft.

Why do astronauts need space suits?

Space suits protect astronauts from the extreme heat and cold of space, and from dangerous radiation. They also give astronauts air to breathe, and stop their bodies from exploding!

How do astronauts repair satellites?

Astronauts repair satellites using the smallest of all manned spacecraft – the Manned Manoeuvring Unit (MMU). The astronaut straps on the MMU, and flies through space, using 24 small jets of gas.

MMU in action

Why do things float around in space?

You don't float around here on Earth, because gravity is always pulling you towards the Earth's surface. In outer space, far away from other worlds, there's no gravity, so everything floats around, including astronauts!

True or False?

Astronauts' helmets are made of gold.

TRUE. At least the visors are. A gold tint protects astronauts' eyes from very strong sunlight.

There's rubbish in space.

TRUE. There are thousands of disused satellites and other dangerous pieces of junk whizzing around the Earth.

Saturn 5 rocket

Why are rockets so huge?

Rockets have to travel very quickly to escape the Earth's atmosphere and reach space. They need huge rocket engines and thousands of tonnes of fuel to reach high speed. Saturn 5 rockets were as high as a 25-storey skyscraper!

Are rockets re-usable?

Most rockets aren't re-usable. When they've run out of fuel, they drop away, never to be used again. But the space shuttle uses two re-usable rocket boosters, which parachute back to Earth.

Shuttle launch

Are rockets all in one piece?

Rockets are made up of several pieces, or stages. The lower stages contain fuel and rocket engines. When they run out of fuel, they're no longer needed. So each empty stage drops away, one by one.

True or False?

Rockets only travel in space.

FALSE. The Blue Flame was a record-breaking rocket car, which could travel at over 1,000 kph – as fast as a jet plane!

Stages crash back to Earth.

FALSE. Rocket stages get very hot as they return to Earth. They burn up, until there's nothing left.

Who first landed on the Moon?

American astronaut Neil Armstrong was the first person to set foot on the Moon in 1969. He landed his Eagle spacecraft, and, along with Buzz Aldrin, spent about two and a half hours exploring the rocky surface, before flying back home.

Moon rock

What did astronauts find on the Moon?

Astronauts collected Moon rocks and soil, and brought them back to Earth to be studied. Two astronauts even found an unmanned probe, which had been sent to the Moon two years earlier.

Who drove a car on the Moon?

A team of astronauts in 1971 drove around on the Moon in a Lunar Rover car. They were able to explore much further than on foot, and collect plenty of rocks.

True or False?

An astronaut played golf on the Moon.

TRUE. Alan Shepard hit golf balls on the Moon. They flew for hundreds of metres because of the Moon's low gravity.

Astronauts left their equipment on the Moon.

TRUE. Astronauts had to leave behind cameras, flags and even the Lunar Rover!

What can you see from the Moon?

The sky over the Moon is always black. The Earth seems very large and bright, as it rises and sets over the horizon. You can also see the Sun and the stars.

Apollo 13

Who didn't make it to the Moon?

There was an explosion aboard the Apollo 13 spacecraft, during a trip to the Moon. The crew were ordered to return to Earth. They only just made it home before they ran out of air.

How long did it take to reach the Moon?

Our nearest neighbour, the Moon, is about 384,000 km from the Earth. Even with the help of fast and powerful rockets, astronauts had to sit in their spacecraft for four and a half days before they reached the Moon.

True or False?

The Moon is covered in water.

FALSE. The Moon has several 'seas' but they're full of rocks and dust, not water. But scientists think there might be frozen water at the Moon's poles.

Russian astronauts have visited the Moon.

FALSE. Twelve astronauts have walked on the Moon – all of them were American.

Astronauts on the Mir space station

How do you eat in space?

Astronauts take dried food into space. They add water, to turn it into a proper meal. You have to eat carefully in space, in case your food floats off the plate!

Can people live in space?

People have stayed in space stations for over a year, but space travel can be bad for your health. Astronauts' bones, hearts and muscles become weak unless they take plenty of exercise.

Inside the Spacelab space station

What happens when space stations close down?

Once space stations are abandoned, they usually fall back to Earth, and burn up in the atmosphere. But the American Skylab space station didn't burn up, and parts of it fell on to farmland in Australia.

Skylab burning up

True or False?

Astronauts need to be strapped down.

TRUE. Astronauts need to be strapped to their beds, otherwise they would float away when they fell asleep!

Astronauts get space sick.

TRUE. Sailors sometimes get seasick, and astronauts can get space sick. They aren't allowed on a space-walk, until they're feeling better.

Space shuttle

Which spacecraft can be used again?

Early spacecraft could only be used once, but the American space shuttle and the Russian Buran spaceplane were designed to be used many times. Six space shuttles have been built. Between them, they have made over 100 space flights.

What is the shuttle used for?

Early shuttle missions carried large satellites into space. But after the shuttle Challenger exploded in 1986, scientists thought it would be safer to use unmanned rockets to launch satellites. These days, the shuttle is used for satellite repair, building a space station and finding out more about space.

What is a robot arm?

The shuttle has a 15 m-long arm, which is used to grab satellites and other objects in space, and put them into the shuttle. Just like your arms, it has shoulder, elbow and wrist joints. Astronauts can even hitch a ride on the arm!

True or False?

The shuttle has piggybacks.

TRUE. When the shuttle needs to get from one side of America to the other, it has to take a piggyback on a Boeing 747 Jumbo Jet.

The shuttle can land on other planets.

FALSE. The shuttle was built to orbit the Earth. It can't land on, or take off from, other planets.

Who landed in the sea?

Astronauts on all the early American space missions parachuted into the sea in their capsules. Navy ships or helicopters kept in touch with the astronauts, collected them, and took them safely back to shore.

What is mission control?

Mission control is the name for the team of scientists and space experts on Earth, who control every space mission. Mission control talks to astronauts by radio, giving them orders and helping out in emergencies.

Mission control

? How do spacecraft return to Earth?

Spacecraft get very hot when they enter the Earth's atmosphere. The shuttle is covered in heat-proof tiles to protect it. It lands on a runway, just like a normal aeroplane.

Shuttle returning to Earth

True or False?

Yuri Gagarin parachuted back to Earth.

TRUE. Yuri Gagarin ejected from his space capsule and floated to the ground using a parachute.

The shuttle is a glider.

TRUE. The shuttle glides back to the ground. This is because it has run out of fuel.

Pathfinder probe

What used balloons to land on Mars?

The Pathfinder probe parachuted on to Mars inside some balloons. When the balloons deflated, a robot car called Sojourner drove away over them.

What is a space probe?

A space probe is an unmanned spacecraft, which sends pictures of other planets and their moons back to Earth. Some probes, such as Pathfinder, land on other planets. The Voyager probes flew past the planets, and are now heading towards the stars.

Giotto probe

Which probe chased a comet?

The Giotto probe chased Halley's comet when it passed Earth in 1986. Giotto proved that the comet was a large, dirty snowball, orbiting the Sun. To protect it from the comet's long, dusty tail, Giotto had a special shield.

Voyager probe

True or False?

Probes get lost in space.

TRUE. Several Mars probes exploded, crashed or missed the planet. Some probes simply went missing.

Pioneer carries a message.

TRUE. Pioneer carries a map of where it came from, and a picture of a man and a woman. Maybe aliens will find it and visit us!

Is there a space telescope?

The Hubble space telescope was launched by a space shuttle in 1990. On Earth, the view of the stars is often spoilt by pollution and street lights. In space, Hubble doesn't have these problems, so it sends us amazing pictures.

Hubble space telescope

Eagle Nebula

What can Hubble see?

The Hubble space telescope can see a very long way into space. It has taken pictures of the Eagle Nebula – a massive cloud of gas. Inside the fingers of cloud, the gas is gathering together to make new stars. Hubble is so sensitive, it could spot a coin 640 km away!

True or False?

Hubble needed to wear glasses.

TRUE. Hubble couldn't see very well at first. Astronauts gave it new lenses, which work like glasses, and it can see much better now.

Hubble has seen alien spacecraft.

FALSE. Hubble has taken pictures of stars in distant parts of the Universe, but it hasn't found any sign of alien life.

How can I become an astronaut?

You have to train for several years to become an astronaut. Here on Earth, astronauts practise space-walking in water tanks. This gives them an idea of how floating in space will feel.

What will spacecraft look like in the future?

The space shuttle is very expensive to launch. American scientists think that the VentureStar space plane might be cheaper. VentureStar could be used to launch other spacecraft in orbit.

VentureStar

Underwater training

Will there be cities in space?

One day, spacecraft might be used to build cities or even hotels in space. Once the International Space Station has been built, it will be a permanent home for astronauts.

International Space Station

True or False?

You can take your holidays in space.

FALSE. Not yet, but maybe one day soon. Unfortunately, a day's holiday in space would cost as much as a house.

You can travel at the speed of light.

FALSE. Even if you could, it would take over four years to reach the next star in our galaxy.

Huygens probe

Is there life on other planets?

Scientists are sure there isn't life on any planet near Earth. But there might be on one of Saturn's moons – Titan. The Huygens probe will parachute on to Titan in 2004 to look for any signs of life.

Will people ever live on other planets?

It might be possible for robots to build airtight buildings on Mars. People could live inside, and grow plants, which would make air and water. Gradually people would be able to live anywhere on the planet.

Mars base of the future

Will we ever travel to other stars?

If a space rocket was sent to the nearest star to our Sun, the journey would last over 150,000 years. We will probably never travel to other stars.

Spacecraft of the future

True or False?

Scientists discovered Martian life.

FALSE. But scientists once thought, wrongly, that some crystals inside a rock from Mars were fossils.

There are very tall volcanoes on Mars.

TRUE. The biggest volcano on Mars is 25 km high – nearly three times higher than Mount Everest, Earth's highest peak.

Questions and Answers about

Long, Long Ago

WHY WERE MAMMOTHS WOOLLY? and other questions about prehistoric animals

WHICH DINOSAUR WAS A BIGHEAD?
and other questions about dinosaurs

WHO WERE THE FIRST PEOPLE?
and other questions about early people

HOW WERE MUMMIES MADE?
and other questions about early civilizations

Why were mammoths woolly?

and other questions about prehistoric animals

Fossil

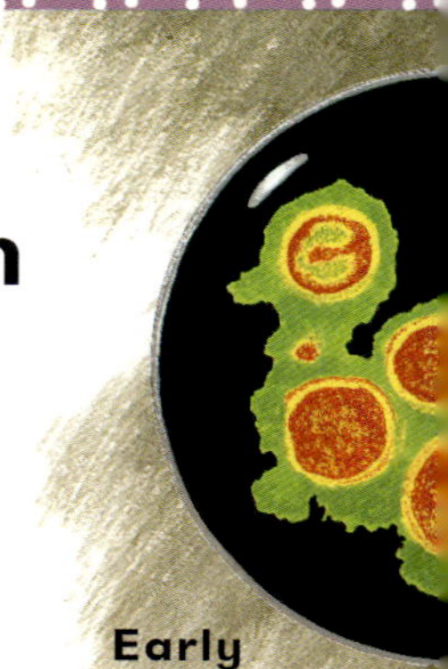

Early bacteria

When did life on Earth begin?

The first-known living things appeared in the oceans about 3,500 million years ago. That's just over 1,000 million years after Earth itself formed.

How do we know about prehistoric life?

Scientists find out about things that lived such a long time ago by studying fossils, the stony remains of ancient life forms.

Stromatolites

What was early life like?

The first living things were microscopically tiny bacteria. Each one was a single living unit called a cell, and hundreds of them would have fitted on this full stop. Sometimes, layer upon layer of the tiny cells build up in shallow water, creating big mounds that scientists call stromatolites.

True or False?

Life might have begun even earlier.

TRUE. It may have started 4,000 million years ago, but scientists haven't found any fossils to prove this.

People used to think Earth formed 6,000 years ago.

TRUE. In 1650, an Irish archbishop said that the Bible showed Earth was created in 4004 BC.

When did the first bigger creatures appear?

Life on Earth evolved slowly, and the first-known multi-celled sea creatures didn't appear until about 800 million years ago. They had no bones or shells, and they looked a bit like worms and jellyfish.

Soft-bodied creatures on the sea bed 800 million years ago

Creatures in the sea 550 million years ago

Why did animals grow shells?

The first-known sea animals with shells began to appear about 550 million years ago. Shells are rather like armour, protecting soft-bodied creatures from attack by enemies. One of the biggest and fiercest of the early animals was Anomalocaris, at about 60 cm long.

True or False?

Some early creatures were longer than your arm.

TRUE. Some grew to as long as a metre.

Early animals had no legs.

FALSE. Animals with legs appeared at about the same time as shelled animals. Hallucigenia had stilt-like legs and spines on its back.

Sacabambaspis

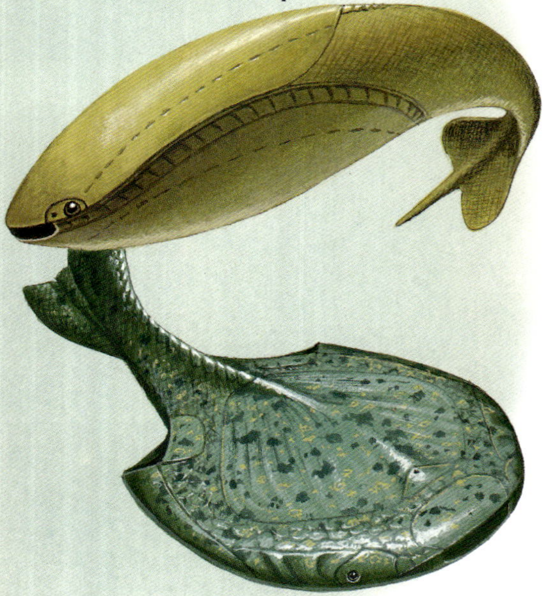

Drepanaspis

What were the first fish like?

Fish had appeared in the oceans by 500 million years ago. They were the first animals to have a proper backbone, but they had no fins, and looked a bit like tadpoles. Fish with jaws and teeth came along a few million years later.

Which fish was as big as a car?

Dunkleosteus was a 3.5 m-long killing machine. Its head was protected by armour-like bony plates, while more bony plates lined its jaws. These were razor sharp – all the better to bite you with!

Dunkleosteus

Stethacanthus

Which shark was rough and ready?

Stethacanthus was a weird early shark with rough, toothlike bristles on top of its head. The top of the T-shaped fin on its back was covered with rough bristles, too.

True or False?

All sharks have bones.

FALSE. Instead of bone, a shark's skeleton is made of tough, bendy stuff called cartilage.

Stethacanthus was a bigger fish than Dunkleosteus.

FALSE. At 70 cm long, Stethacanthus was only one-fifth the size of the monster Dunkleosteus.

Which were the first land animals?

The first-known landlubbers were small spiders, millipedes and insects. By 300 million years ago there were dragonflies the size of kites, and millipedes twice as long as a bicycle!

What were the first four-legged animals like?

Backboned land animals, such as Ichthyostega, evolved about 370 million years ago, from fish whose fins had become legs. They could crawl on to land, and they could breathe underwater too.

Ichthyostega

Why did early land animals stay near water?

Ichthyostega and Acanthostega were ancestors of the amphibians, animals that lay their jelly-like eggs in water, and whose young live in water and have gills. As amphibians become adults, they lose their gills and develop lungs. They can live on land, but their skin and their eggs have to be kept damp, so they need to stay close to water.

Acanthostega

True or False?

Animals appeared on land long before plants.

FALSE. Land plants came first. The first with roots and a stem was Cooksonia, from about 420 million years ago.

Insects were the first animals to fly.

TRUE. The first in the air were giant dragonflies like Meganeura.

When did animals get away from water?

By 300 million years ago, a new animal group had evolved. These were the reptiles – animals that can live away from water because their skin is dry and scaly, and because their eggs are protected from drying out by a leathery shell. The small, lizard-like Hylonomus was one of the first.

Dimetrodon

What were the sailbacks?

The sailbacks were reptiles and, like other reptiles, they were cold-blooded, with bodies that rely on the Sun's heat to warm them. Scientists think the sail-like fins on their backs worked rather like solar panels, soaking up heat. At 3 m from head to tail tip, Dimetrodon was as long as a car.

True or False?

All early reptiles were small animals.

FALSE. The plant-eating Pareiasaurus was about the same size as a cow.

Sailbacks also used their fins to cool down.

TRUE. Scientists think the fins could lose heat as well as take it in.

Where did dinosaurs come from?

Dinosaurs evolved from a group called the ruling reptiles, which appeared about 250 million years ago – about 20 million years before the first dinosaurs.

Where did crocodiles come from?

There's a good reason why today's crocodiles look a lot like early ruling reptiles – they also evolved from them. Scientists think one of the earliest, Deinosuchus, grew to a massive 15m – three times as long as today's biggest crocodiles.

What was special about ruling reptiles?

Early ones like Chasmatosaurus walked on all fours, but over time some ruling reptiles raised themselves up and began to walk on their back legs. The next stage after speedy, two-legged ruling reptiles like Lagosuchus was the dinosaur!

True or False?

All of the reptiles lived on dry land.

FALSE. Although reptiles had evolved to live on dry land, some of them went back to the water.

Snakes came along before the dinosaurs.

FALSE. Modern snakes evolved about 20 million years ago, long after the dinosaurs died out.

Who ruled the skies in dinosaur times?

At about the same time as the first dinosaurs appeared, some reptiles evolved wings. These flying reptiles are called pterosaurs, and their wings were flaps of skin.

What did pterosaurs eat?

Some pterosaurs snapped up insects, while others dived down to the sea to scoop up fish. Pterodaustro probably sieved tiny sea creatures through the bristly teeth in its lower jaw, much as flamingoes do today. Dsungaripterus may have used the tip of its curved beak to prize shellfish off rocks.

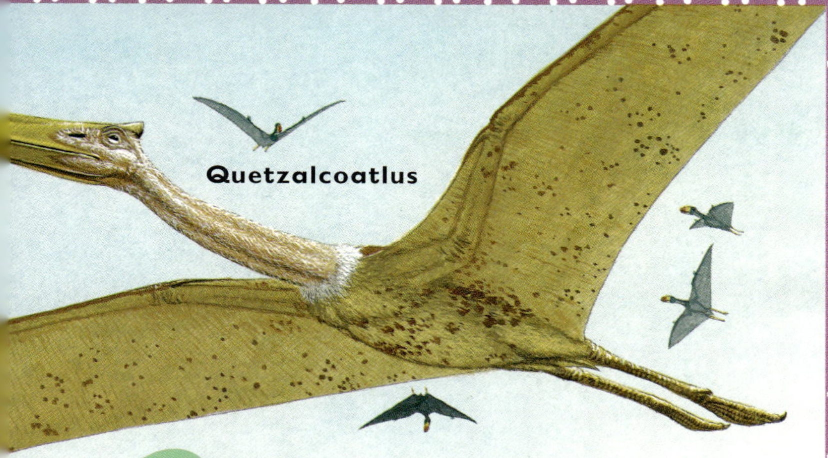

Quetzalcoatlus

Which pterosaur was as big as a hang-glider?

The biggest pterosaur of all was Quetzalcoatlus. Scientists think its outspread wings measured a whopping 40 feet – that gave it the biggest wings the world has ever known!

Pterodactylus

True or False?

Pterosaurs had feathers.

FALSE. Most had furry bodies and leathery wings, as bats do today.

Some reptiles can fly today.

TRUE. There's a lizard that can glide on wing-like flaps of skin. There were lizard-like gliding reptiles in prehistoric times, too.

Who ruled the waves in dinosaur times?

While some reptiles took to the air, others went back to the oceans. By dinosaur times, three of the main groups were sea turtles, ichthyosaurs and the long-necked plesiosaurs.

Which turtle was bigger than a rowboat?

Archelon was more than 11 feet long. Scientists think it ate jellyfish – it must have eaten truck-loads before it was full!

Which plesiosaur had the longest neck?

If people had been around in Elasmosaurus's time, there would have been room for seven swimmers to lie on this giant plesiosaur's back – more than four of them on its 26 feet-long neck!

True or False?

Plesiosaurs died out at the same time as the dinosaurs.

TRUE. The big sea reptiles died out 65 million years ago, as did the pterosaurs.

Plesiosaurs breathed underwater.

FALSE. The sea reptiles had to surface to breathe air, just as dolphins and whales do today.

What came after the dinosaurs?

After the dinosaurs died out 65 million years ago, another group of animals, the mammals, began to take over. One of the special things about this group is that mammals feed their young on mother's milk. No other animals do this. Mammals evolved from reptiles, and they appeared about 220 million years ago. One of the earliest, Megazostrodon, was a little bigger than a mouse.

Zalambdalestes

Megazostrodon

Did early mammals lay eggs?

Although their young sucked milk, the first mammal mothers laid eggs. Over time, new kinds of mammal began to give birth to live young, just as most mammals do today. Egg-laying mammals are still around, though – Australia's duck-billed platypus is the most famous.

True or False?

Mammals are warm-blooded.

TRUE. Unlike amphibians, fish and reptiles, they can make their own body heat.

Kangaroos are mammals.

TRUE. They're marsupials – mammals whose babies grow up in the mother's pouch. Marsupials appeared about 100 million years ago.

Icaronycteris

Which were the first flying mammals?

Bats are still the only mammals that can flap their wings to fly. Unlike modern bats, though, the earliest-known bat had a long tail. It is called Icaronycteris, and it appeared about 54 million years ago.

Dinornis

Which was the tallest bird?

At 11 feet high, and a lot larger than a modern-day camel, Dinornis was the tallest bird that has ever lived. It belonged to a group of flightless New Zealand birds called moas, which died out about 200 years ago.

What were the first whales like?

Whales, dolphins and seals are some of the mammals that developed ways of living in water. The earliest-known whale, Pakicetus, appeared at about the same time as the bats, and looked more like a seal than a modern whale.

Pakicetus

True or False?

Some mammals can glide.

TRUE. Planetetherium was a prehistoric mammal that could glide.

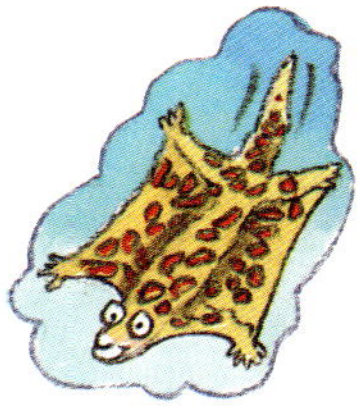

Dinornis was the first bird.

FALSE. Dinornis appeared about 2 million years ago, but the earliest-known bird, Archaeopteryx, lived about 150 million years ago.

What were saber-toothed cats like?

Their two huge fangs made saber-tooths like Smilodon some of the fiercest cats that have ever lived. They could open their mouths really wide so they could stab their teeth into victims.

Which animals attacked saber-tooths?

Packs of early wolves, called dire wolves, were brave enough to take on saber-tooths. Scientists have found fossils of their bones covered in each other's teeth marks. Dire wolves and saber-tooths lived about 25,000 years ago.

Dire wolves

How big were the first bears?

Agriotherium lived about 5 million years ago. At 6 feet long, it was about the same size as a modern grizzly bear.

Agriotherium

True or False?

Dogs appeared 40 million years ago.

TRUE. But the earliest ones like Phlaocyon looked more like raccoons than the dogs you see today.

Cats appeared 40 million years ago.

FALSE. They first appeared on Earth about 35 million years ago.

Which was the biggest-ever land mammal?

Indricotherium

Indricotherium was as heavy as four elephants and 1.5 times the height of a modern giraffe. Although it looked like a cross between them, it was an early kind of rhinoceros.

Which was the ugliest mammal?

Eobasileus

Lots of prehistoric animals looked very strange in comparison to modern animals. With its lumpy, bumpy head, one of the weirdest-looking was Eobasileus.

Which deer had branch-sized antlers?

Megaloceros's antlers were massive – at 12 feet across, they were wider than its body was long.

True or False?

Some prehistoric mammals climbed trees.

TRUE. Primates were a mammal group that learned to climb trees. Over millions of years, they evolved into apes, monkeys and humans.

There were giant beavers in prehistoric times.

TRUE. Castoroides was bear-sized.

When were horses the size of foxes?

The earliest-known horse, Hyracotherium, had toes instead of hooves, and was only about 8 inches high. It evolved about 50 million years ago, and lived in forests, where its size helped it to hide from meat-eaters. Equus, the kind of horse we know today, didn't appear until about 5 million years ago.

When were elephants the size of pigs?

When the first elephants appeared about 40 million years ago, they were tiny. Moeritherium, for example, was only about 2 feet high. All sorts of strange-looking kinds evolved before the ancestors of modern elephants appeared about 5 million years ago.

Moeritherium

Deinotherium

Platybelodon

Anancus

True or False?

Elephants were the only animals to have trunks.

FALSE. Macrauchenia looked like a cross between a camel, a rhinoceros and an elephant.

Horses were once attacked by birds.

TRUE. They had to watch out for the flightless bird Diatryma – it was 10 times as tall as them.

Why were mammoths woolly?

A mammoth's thick woolly fur was like a jumper, helping it to keep warm. Mammoths needed this extra layer because they lived during the Ice Ages – times when Earth's weather was so freezing cold that snow and ice spread down from the North Pole over Europe and North America.

Woolly mammoths

Why did mammoths die out?

The last Ice Age began to end when the weather became warmer again about 12,000 years ago. Lots of animals died out at this time, including woolly mammoths and woolly rhinoceroses. Scientists think this happened partly because these animals couldn't cope with the warmer weather, but also because they were hunted by a new kind of mammal – human beings!

True or False?

Scientists have found frozen mammoths.

TRUE. In 1977, they even found a baby mammoth's body in the frozen ground of Siberia. It died 40,000 years ago.

All mammoths were big.

FALSE. Mini-mammoths lived on an island in the Arctic Ocean. They died out about 6,000 years ago.

Which dinosaur was a bighead?

and other questions about dinosaurs

How big were the biggest dinosaurs?

Long-necked dinosaurs, such as Brachiosaurus, were massive. Measuring more than 22 m from head to tail, and weighing well over 30 tonnes, this dinosaur was about as long as a tennis court and heavier than five elephants. It was tall enough to peer over the top of a four-storey house!

Brachiosaurus

How small were the smallest dinosaurs?

Some dinosaurs were tiny. At about 1 m long, for example, Compsognathus wasn't much larger than a turkey!

Compsognathus

True or False?

Brachiosaurus was the biggest dinosaur of all.

FALSE. Other long-necked dinosaurs were even larger – Argentinosaurus may have been twice as big.

Dinosaurs were the biggest animals ever.

FALSE. The blue whale is the biggest animal ever, at 130 tonnes.

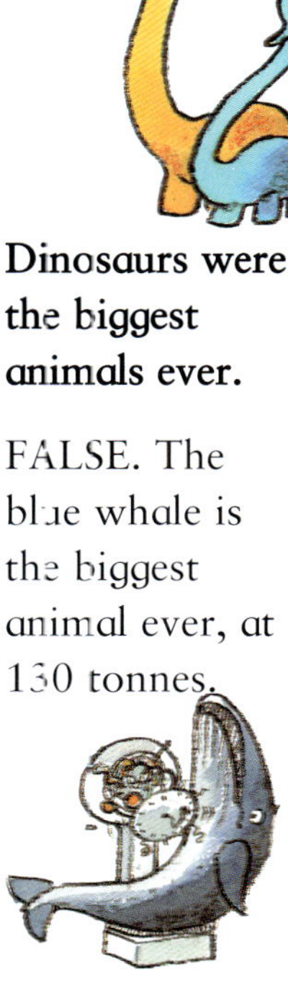

How many kinds of dinosaur were there?

Dinosaurs were around for millions of years, and all sorts of different kinds developed. Scientists have now named about 800 dinosaurs, but there may have been twice as many kinds altogether.

When did dinosaurs live?

The very first kinds of dinosaur appeared on Earth about 225 million years ago. One of the earliest was Herrerasaurus, a meat-eater that lived in the area we now call Argentina.

What sort of animal were they?

Dinosaurs were reptiles, but they were a bit different from other reptiles such as lizards, crocodiles and tortoises. Dinosaurs held their legs straight under their bodies – unlike other reptiles, whose legs sprawl out to the side.

True or False?

Dinosaurs could fly.

FALSE. They were land animals. Other creatures ruled the air and the seas.

Dinosaur babies hatched from eggs.

TRUE. Like other reptiles, dinosaurs laid eggs.

How do we know about dinosaurs?

No one knows exactly what dinosaurs were like because, about 65 million years ago, they all suddenly died out. Scientists work like detectives to piece bits of information together, and their main clues are fossils – the stony remains of living things that died a very long time ago.

How were fossils made?

Sometimes a dead animal would sink to the bottom of a river, lake or sea, where it was covered by sand or mud. Over millions of years, the sand and mud became rock, and the animal's bones turned into fossils.

What kind of dinosaur fossils do scientists find?

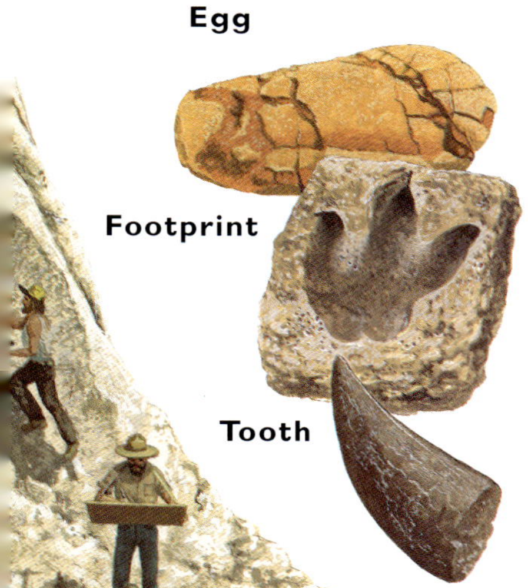

The most common dinosaur fossils formed from hard body parts such as bones and teeth. Sometimes, though, scientists find fossils of dinosaur eggs or droppings, or rocks that show the pattern of their skin or footprints.

True or False?

Only animals can turn into stony fossils.

FALSE. Trees and other plants can turn into fossils, too.

Children can find fossils.

TRUE. One of the earliest fossil-hunters was Mary Anning, who made her first big find in 1810, when she was twelve.

What did dinosaurs eat?

Most dinosaurs ate plants. There were lots of fierce and hungry meat-eaters, though, and they ate anything they could catch, including other dinosaurs!

Why do scientists love dinosaur droppings?

It's lucky that fossils don't smell, because scientists study fossilised dinosaur droppings to find out about the kind of things dinosaurs liked to eat.

Did dinosaurs eat grass?

No, not even plant-eating dinosaurs ate grass, because these plants didn't appear until long after the dinosaurs died out. Plant-eating dinosaurs mainly ate ferns and early kinds of tree, such as the palm-like cycad, and pine trees.

True or False?

Dinosaurs ate flowers.

TRUE. Flowers first appeared about 135 million years ago, so the later dinosaurs may have liked eating them.

Some dinosaurs were cannibals.

TRUE. Scientists have discovered a fossilised Coelophysis that had eaten its own babies.

Who was king of the dinosaurs?

Rex means 'king', and Tyrannosaurus means 'tyrant lizard' (a tyrant is a cruel, powerful ruler). Scientists named Tyrannosaurus rex because they thought it was big and mean enough to rule over all other animals, killing and eating anything it fancied. At about 12 m, it was bus-sized, with a huge head and a mouth big enough to gulp you down whole.

Tyrannosaurus rex

Giganotosaurus

Who was the giant dinosaur?

Giganotosaurus means 'giant southern lizard', and scientists think that this meat-eater was even bigger than Tyrannosaurus!

What colour was Tyrannosaurus?

No one has found a fossil that shows what colour any of the dinosaurs were. Scientists think that some were brightly coloured, while others were patterned to match their surroundings – just as many animals are today.

True or False?

Tyrannosaurus could run as fast as a car.

FALSE. No dinosaurs could run that fast, but Tyrannosaurus could still have run a lot faster than you do!

Tyrannosaurus left enormous droppings.

TRUE. Scientists have found a fossil of a loaf-sized dropping, which probably came from a Tyrannosaurus.

Which dinosaur went fishing?

At about 10.5 m long, Baryonyx was a big dinosaur with crocodile-like jaws. Scientists think it ate fish, snapping them up in its mouth or hooking them up out of the water with its thumb claws, just as grizzly bears do today.

Which dinosaur had a sail on its back?

No one is certain what the sail-like structure on Spinosaurus's back was for. It may have been used like a flag to signal to other dinosaurs, or it may have worked a bit like a solar panel to help Spinosaurus heat up or cool down.

Spinosaurus

Who was the biggest fish-eater?

Suchomimus was at least a metre longer than its cousin Baryonyx, and probably grew to as long as the 12-m Tyrannosaurus.

True or False?

Spinosaurus was destroyed during World War II.

TRUE. Its fossils were blown up in a bombing raid.

Suchomimus was a bigger dinosaur than Spinosaurus.

FALSE. Scientists think Spinosaurus grew to as long as 17 m.

Which dinosaur had a long big toenail?

Velociraptor was one of the scariest dinosaurs in the 1993 movie Jurassic Park. This dinosaur didn't just have sharp teeth and vicious clawed hands. Even more frightening was the huge curved claw on each foot – when Velociraptor attacked, it could swing these claws forwards, to slash at its prey.

Velociraptors

Are model dinosaurs true to life?

The model dinosaurs in Jurassic Park were incredibly realistic, but some were a little larger than life. The Velociraptors, for example, looked more like their cousin, Deinonychus. At about 3 m long, this dinosaur was almost twice the size of Velociraptor. And another cousin, Utahraptor, was twice as big as Deinonychus!

True or False?

Velociraptor and its cousins used to hunt in packs.

TRUE. It helped them to kill dinosaurs a lot bigger than themselves.

Only these sorts of dinosaur were pack hunters.

FALSE. Other meat-eating dinosaurs, such as Coelophysis, also hunted in packs.

Which dinosaurs cracked a whip?

The huge plant-eating dinosaurs didn't just have long necks – some of them also had incredibly long tails. Apatosaurus, Barosaurus and Diplodocus may have flicked their extra-long tails like a whip, making an incredibly loud noise to scare away their enemies.

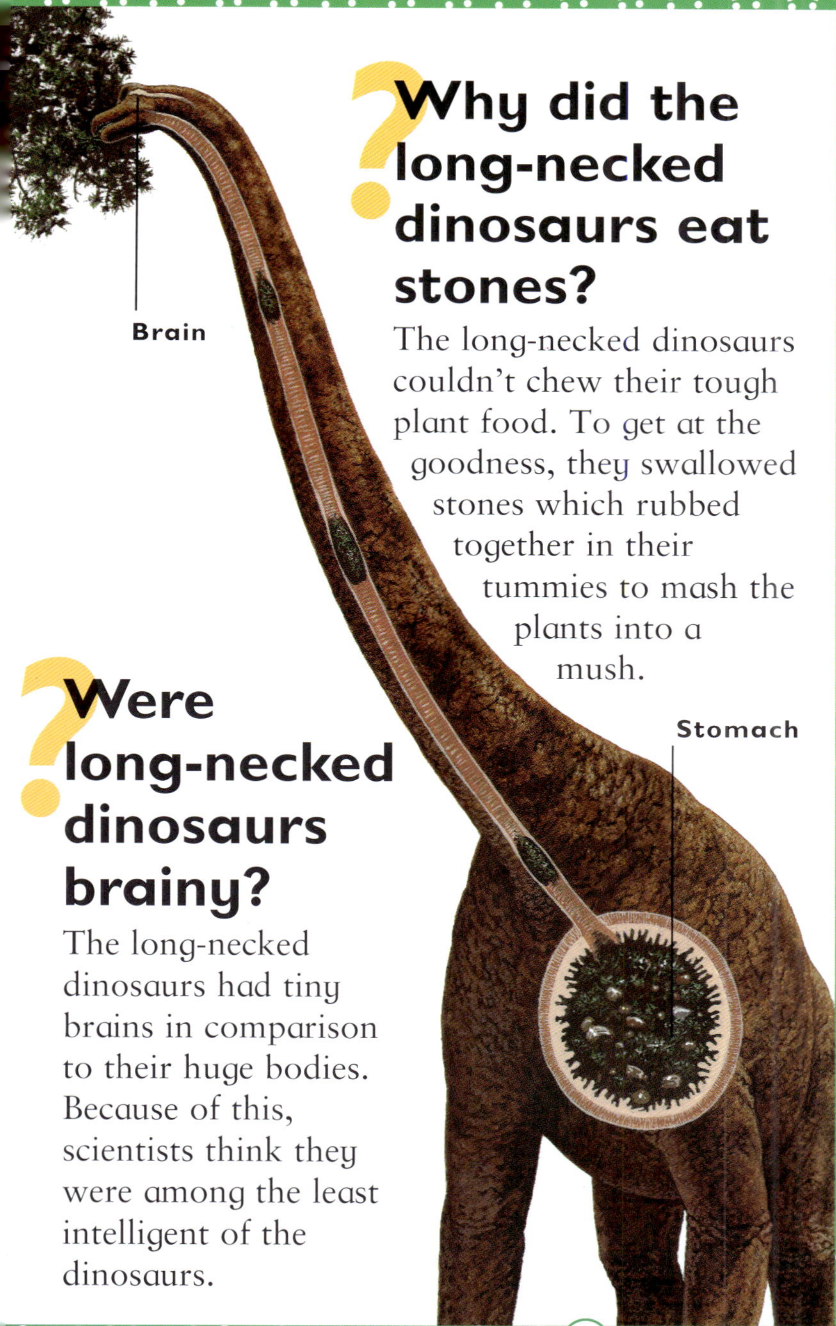

Why did the long-necked dinosaurs eat stones?

The long-necked dinosaurs couldn't chew their tough plant food. To get at the goodness, they swallowed stones which rubbed together in their tummies to mash the plants into a mush.

Were long-necked dinosaurs brainy?

The long-necked dinosaurs had tiny brains in comparison to their huge bodies. Because of this, scientists think they were among the least intelligent of the dinosaurs.

True or False?

Long-necked dinosaurs were very greedy.

TRUE. They were so big that to stay alive, they had to spend nearly all their time eating.

Tyrannosaurus rex was the brainiest dinosaur.

FALSE. It was brainier than long-necked dinosaurs, but not as smart as a Velociraptor.

Which dinosaurs had duckbills?

Parasaurolophus, Corythosaurus and Lambeosaurus belonged to a group of plant-eating dinosaurs called duckbills – named because their mouths ended in a toothless beak, or bill. When predators threatened them, they could run away on two legs, and may have rushed into the water to escape.

Who liked to blow his own trumpet?

Parasaurolophus had a weird, hollow crest bone, which it may have blown through like a trumpet. Scientists made a model of the bone, and found it produced a low booming sound.

Who was the helmet lizard?

Corythosaurus means 'helmet lizard', even though this dinosaur's crest looked more like a dinner plate than a helmet! Scientists think the duckbilled dinosaurs used their crests to show off when trying to attract a mate.

True or False?

Dinosaurs with crests could breathe underwater.

FALSE. Scientists once thought crests worked like snorkels. Then they realised there were no air-holes at the top!

Duckbilled dinosaurs had no teeth.

FALSE. They had rows of teeth behind their beaks.

Were dinosaurs good parents?

Maiasaura means 'good mother lizard', and scientists named this dinosaur because they found it beside a nest full of its babies. Other kinds of dinosaur may have also stayed with their young, feeding and protecting them.

Which dinosaur laid the biggest egg?

Some of the biggest eggs found so far belonged to a long-necked dinosaur called Hypselosaurus. They were about 30 cm long – roughly the same size as a rugby ball.

Which of the dinosaurs was an egg robber?

Oviraptor means 'egg robber', and this dinosaur also got its name because it was discovered near a nest. Scientists used to think it was about to steal the eggs when it died. Later they found a fossilised Oviraptor that had died protecting its own nest, proving it was a good parent, after all.

True or False?

Dinosaur eggs were first found in the 1800s.

FALSE. The first eggs were found in the 1920s. They belonged to a Protoceratops.

Dinosaurs used to nest in trees.

FALSE. They made their nests on the ground. Some nests were holes, others were built up into mounds.

Why did Triceratops have horns?

Triceratops was like a giant rhinoceros – as heavy as an elephant and as long as a truck. Even though it looked so fierce, Triceratops was a plant-eater and probably used its horns to scare off meat-eating enemies, such as Tyrannosaurus rex and Velociraptor.

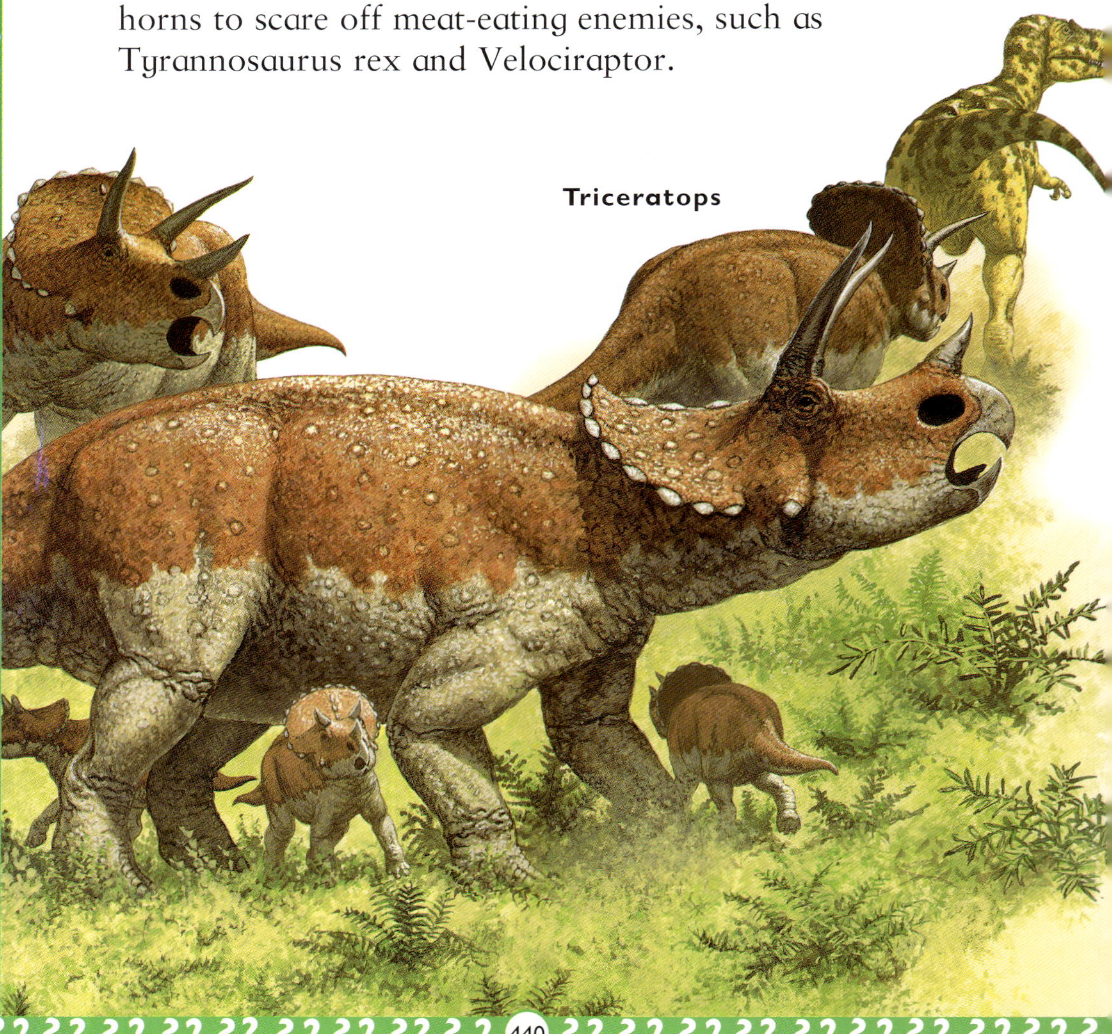

Triceratops

Pachycephalosaurus

Who were headbangers?

Pachycephalosaurus's skull was so thick and tough that scientists think it worked like a crash helmet, and that these dinosaurs fought each other by headbanging.

Pentaceratops

Which dinosaur was a bighead?

Triceratops's head was about 2 m long, but its cousin Pentaceratops's was bigger. At over 3 m, even a car could have parked on it!

True or False?

Triceratops could sharpen its own teeth.

TRUE. When it chewed, its teeth ground together and got sharper.

Dinosaurs only lived in small groups.

FALSE. Some, including Triceratops, lived in large herds made up of dozens of dinosaurs.

Why were some dinosaurs built like tanks?

Some plant-eating dinosaurs, such as Sauropelta, were big bruisers with extra-tough skin covered in bony spikes and bumps. All this armour-plating helped protect them against meat-eaters.

Stegosaurus

Which dinosaur spiked its enemies?

Stegosaurus's tail had vicious spikes at its tip, which were just as dangerous as Triceratops's horns.

Which dinosaur packed a mean punch?

When Euoplocephalus swung its tail, the bumps on its tip worked like a club for bashing its enemies about. Ouch!

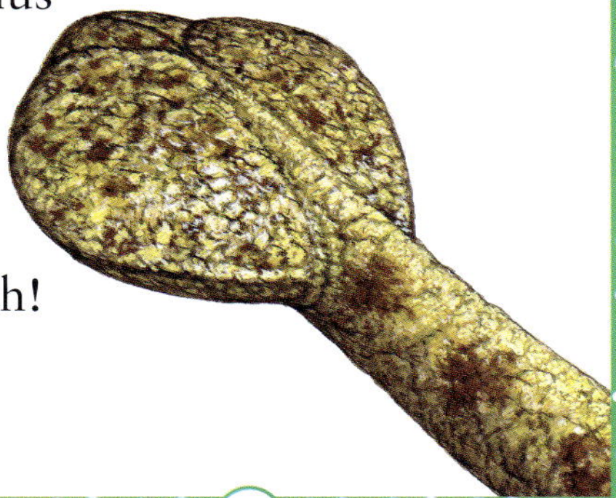

True or False?

Dinosaurs lived in Australia.

TRUE. Scientists have found dinosaur fossils on every continent, including Australia and Antarctica.

Dinosaurs' tails helped them to balance.

TRUE. Holding its tail out behind it helped a running dinosaur keep its balance.

How fast could dinosaurs run?

Scientists think that dinosaurs such as Gallimimus and Struthiomimus were the speediest, and that they could run as fast as ostriches. Ostriches can't fly, but they are the largest birds alive today – with their long, strong legs they can belt across the ground at speeds of up to 65 kph.

Struthiomimus

Archaeopteryx

Fossil of Archaeopteryx

What were dinobirds?

Archaeopteryx was a feathered creature that lived more than 145 million years ago. Many scientists now think that birds are descended from dinosaurs, and that Archaeopteryx was a cross between a bird and a dinosaur – a dinobird!

True or False?

Ostriches were around in dinosaur times.

FALSE. Ostriches didn't appear until a long time after the dinosaurs lived.

Archaeopteryx is the only dinobird found to date.

FALSE. The fossils of the dinobird Caudipteryx, were named in 1998.

What happened to the dinosaurs?

Many scientists think that 65 million years ago, a gigantic chunk of space rock smashed into the Earth. The force of the hit was like an explosion. It threw up huge clouds of dust which blocked out the Sun and plunged the Earth into freezing darkness. Without sunlight, plants couldn't grow, so first the plant-eating dinosaurs died of cold and hunger, then the meat-eaters starved.

Are any dinosaurs alive today?

No dinosaurs survived the disaster, but some birds did. So if scientists are right, and birds are descended from dinosaurs, then their relatives are still alive and hopping today!

True or False?

The space rock that hit Earth was as big as a city.

TRUE. Scientists think it was at least 10 km across.

Scientists think they know where the rock hit the Earth.

TRUE. The Chicxulub crater is a vast hollow in the seabed off Mexico. It formed about 65 million years ago.

Who were the first people?

and other questions about early people

Who were the first people?

The scientific name for people like you and me is Homo sapiens, and our ancestors, the first modern humans, appeared about 180,000 years ago. Experts believe that, like all creatures, we evolved very, very slowly, over millions of years, from earlier kinds of animal.

Lucy **Homo erectus** **Homo sapiens**

Who was Lucy?

The earliest human-like creatures were the Australopithecines, who were evolving as long as 4.5 million years ago. Lucy is the nickname given to a fossilised Australopithecine skeleton found in 1974.

True or False?

Human life first began in Africa.

TRUE. The Australopithecines evolved in Africa, and so did the first human beings.

Lucy was named after a pop song.

True. She was named after 'Lucy in the sky with diamonds' by the Beatles.

What was the Stone Age?

Well over 2.5 million years ago, some bright spark picked up a rock and made a stone tool from it. When experts talk about the Stone Age, they mean the long period of time from making the first stone tools to about 5,000 years ago, when bronze tools were first made.

What were early tools used for?

Homo erectus people chipped stones into sharp hand-axes, which they mainly used for skinning animals and cutting up the meat.

When were weapons invented?

The earliest weapons were pointed wooden sticks used as hunting spears. It's likely that Homo erectus people were the first to make them, more than 400,000 years ago.

True or False?

All Stone Age tools were made of stone.

FALSE. Later in the Stone Age, people made tools from animal bones, antlers and ivory.

Hand-axes didn't have handles.

TRUE. Tools have only had wooden handles in the past 100,000 years or so.

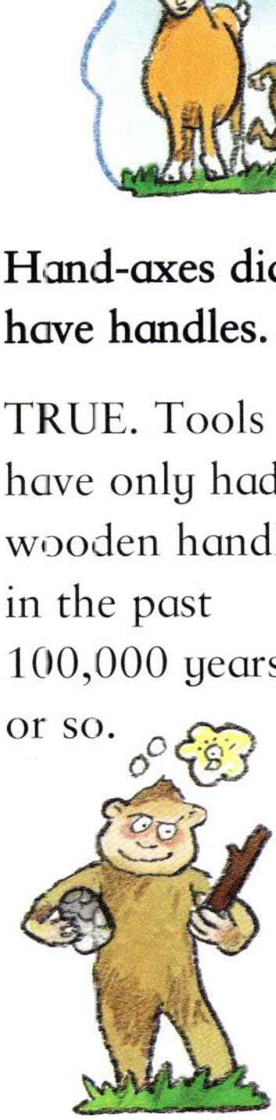

Why were Stone Age people great travellers?

Although the first human-like creatures lived in eastern and southern Africa, by about 1.8 million years ago, Homo erectus people were exploring other lands. It wasn't long before some of them reached southeastern Asia. By 700,000 years ago, others were living in Europe.

Homo erectus people

Who were the first Americans?

Some of our modern human ancestors were living in North America by 15,000 years ago. They were able to walk there from northern Asia because it was once joined to North America by dry land called Beringia.

True or False?

Stone Age people lived in Australia.

TRUE. They were living there by 50,000 years ago.

Stone Age people walked everywhere.

FALSE. We don't know when boats were first made, but people must have used them to travel to Australia.

Which bright sparks lit the first fires?

Experts think that Homo erectus people were the first to toast their toes around a camp fire, perhaps as long as 1.6 million years ago.

Homo erectus family

Why was fire useful?

The weather got colder once Homo erectus headed out of sunny Africa, so fire must have been one way of keeping warm. Stone Age people also cooked over fires and hardened their wooden spear-tips in the flames.

How did Stone Age people light fires?

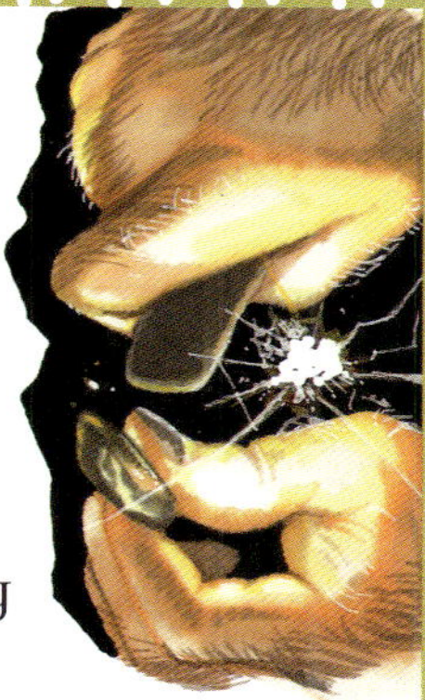

The first fire-makers probably took flames from bush fires started by a flash of lightning. Later on, people sparked off their own fires by rubbing dry sticks together or bashing two stones against each other.

True or False?

Homo erectus people were probably the first to put on clothes.

TRUE. Clothes were another way of keeping warm.

Fire helped to keep Stone Age people out of danger.

TRUE. A blazing branch was a sure-fire way of frightening off fierce animals.

Neanderthals

Who were the Neanderthals?

The Neanderthals were a kind of early human who evolved several thousand years before our modern human ancestors appeared.

Neanderthal man

Were Neanderthal people stupid?

Experts once thought so, but they've changed their minds. The Neanderthals looked different from our ancestors – they were sturdier, with differently shaped heads – but they seem to have been just as skilful.

Neanderthals hunting woolly mammoths

How did Neanderthals hunt with fire?

Some Neanderthals lived through the Ice Ages – long periods of freezing weather when much of Europe and North America was covered in snow and ice. Mammoths were huge, so the Neanderthals had to invent clever ways of killing them, like using burning branches to chase them over cliffs.

True or False?

There are Neanderthals around today.

FALSE. No one knows why, but they died out about 30,000 years ago.

Neanderthals lived in North America.

FALSE. They died out before the first people travelled there.

What other animals did people hunt?

Stone Age hunters went after anything they could catch – from mammoths and rhinoceroses, to herds of reindeer and bison. People who lived by the sea caught seals and fish, while the first Australians hunted giant kangaroos.

How did people cook?

Some time after they learned to use fire, Stone Age people invented spits for cooking roast dinners. Early spits were probably made by pushing a sharp stick through a piece of meat, then balancing the stick on forked twigs.

Did they have cooking pots?

Most Stone Age people didn't. Clay pots weren't made until about 11,000 years ago.

True or False?

Stone Age people ate fruit and vegetables.

TRUE. They gathered all sorts of leaves, roots, berries and nuts.

Stone Age people ate chocolate.

FALSE. There was no sugar either, but they probably stole sweet honey from bees' nests.

Did Stone Age people live in caves?

They did if they were near mountains or cliffs and could find a big enough cave. Stone Age people lived in bands made up of several families, and a small band might have 25 members.

Why did mammoths come in handy?

The people who didn't live near mountains or cliffs built their own shelters. Some were dome-shaped huts made from mammoth bones and tusks.

Mammoth hut

Did Stone Age people build villages?

Not until about 10,000 years ago. Before then, people spent much of their time on the move, looking for food. These kind of travellers are called hunter-gatherers, because they lived by hunting animals and gathering plants to eat.

True or False?

Stone Age people used to build tepees.

TRUE. Some people made tepee-shaped shelters from branches covered in animal skins.

All Stone Age homes were very small.

FALSE. In the later Stone Age, some people were building huts bigger than a tennis court.

Cave painting

Who were the first artists?

Some time around 30,000 years ago, our modern human ancestors began to carve and paint pictures into cave walls and roofs. Most pictures were of the animals they hunted – everything from a charging bison, to a herd of leaping deer.

What paints did they use?

Cave artists used kinds of earth called ochre for yellow, red and brown. Clay or chalky stones gave them white, while burnt twigs gave them charcoal for black. They dabbed the paint on with their fingers, or made brushes by fixing pads of animal fur to sticks. Sometimes they spray-painted by blowing paint through a hollow bone.

Who were the first musicians?

No one knows when music began, but the world's oldest musical instrument is a whistle carved from an animal bone more than 60,000 years ago!

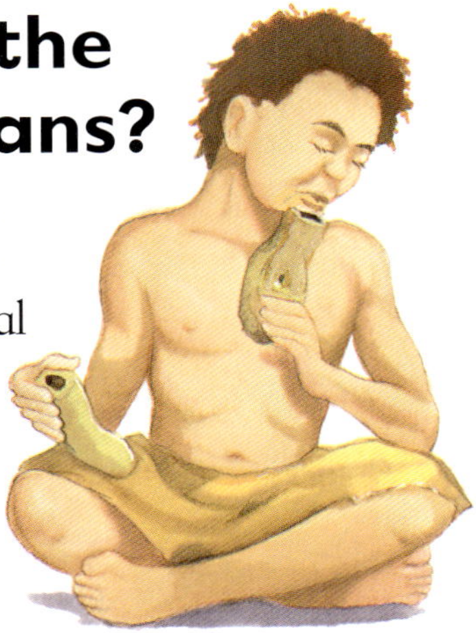

Stone Age musician

True or False?

Early artists used ladders.

TRUE. They must have climbed something to paint pictures on cave roofs.

Cave paintings were Stone Age wallpaper.

FALSE. The pictures weren't decorations. The caves were probably used for magical or religious rituals.

Were Stone Age people religious?

In Stone Age times, anything mysterious or powerful must have seemed like a god or goddess – from the Sun, Moon and stars, to fire, wind, water and animals.

Did they have priests?

We don't know for sure, but some sculptures and cave paintings show mysterious beings that are part-human, part-animal. These may have been early priests who dressed as animals for special ceremonies.

Religious ceremony

Did they have doctors?

Not like the doctors of today, but they did try their hand at operations. People have found 8,000-year-old skulls with holes – Stone Age doctors probably thought illnesses were caused by evil spirits, and cut the neat little holes to let them escape.

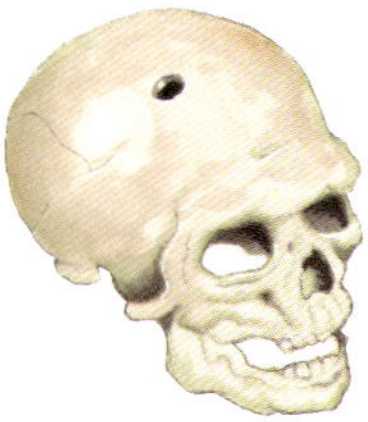

Stone Age skull

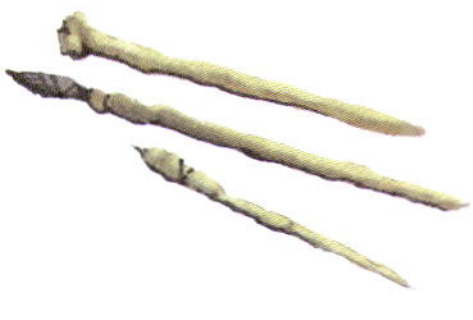

Medical instruments

True or False?

Stone Age people probably believed there was a heaven.

TRUE. Late Stone Age people buried their dead with all sorts of things that would be useful in an afterlife.

They took pills when they were sick.

FALSE. But they probably knew how to use plants to cure things like upset tummies.

How do we know what clothes were like?

Homo sapiens children

We think the first clothes were made from animal skins because we've found tools for cleaning the skins, and we know that looms for weaving cloth weren't invented until about 7,000 years ago.

We haven't found any early clothes, though, because unlike bones or stone tools, leather rots away quickly. Some of the earliest clothing finds came from the graves of people buried in Russia about 25,000 years ago.

Making clothes

Who was the Iceman?

In 1991, a mummified body complete with clothes, weapons and even a backpack was discovered frozen into the ice of the Alps mountains. The mummy was nicknamed the Iceman, and it's one of the oldest ever found. When he died about 5,300 years ago, the Iceman was wearing a leather tunic and shoes, a furry hat and a woven grass cape.

The Iceman

True or False?

Stone Age people wore woolly jumpers.

FALSE. People only began knitting clothes about 3,000 years ago.

Stone Age people invented sewing needles.

TRUE. Sewing needles were being used by early people 25,000 years ago. They were made from bone.

Stone Age necklace

Did people wear jewellery?

People were wearing beautiful jewellery by the time the first cave art was created. Polished stones, shells, ivory and animal teeth were all made into bracelets, necklaces and headbands.

Did they carry lucky charms?

We've also found beautiful small carvings of animals, which people probably carried about with them as lucky charms.

Carved animals may have been toys or charms.

Did they cut their hair?

They probably did, but not with scissors – they weren't invented until long after the Stone Age was over. A 25,000-year-old ivory carving shows a beautiful woman who looks as though her hair was cut into a fringe.

Stone Age woman

True or False?

Stone Age men wore bracelets.

TRUE. We've found skeletons of men who were buried wearing bracelets made from the tusks of mammoths.

Stone Age people made gold jewellery.

FALSE. Copper bracelets were worn 6,000 years ago, but gold jewellery had to wait for another 1,000 years or so.

Who were the first farmers?

In the Middle East by 10,000 years ago, people were settling down. Instead of moving about as hunter-gatherers, they saved wild seeds so they could grow their own crops, and built villages where they could live all the time. Later on, they started to keep animals. Farming had begun.

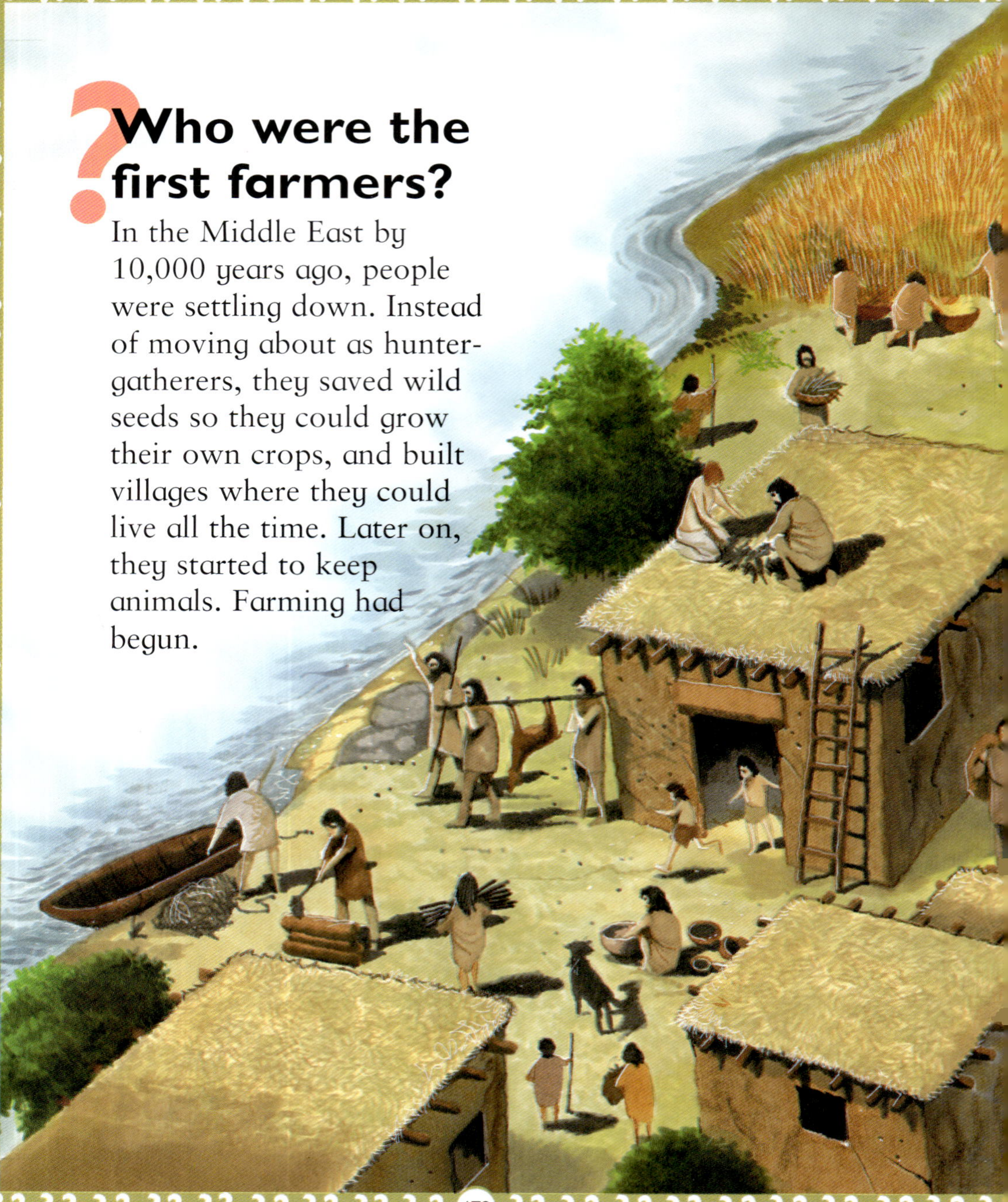

Did they keep cows?

Not at first – goats and sheep were the first animals to be farmed. Pigs and cows were tamed and farmed a while later.

Did they have pets?

Dogs have long been people's best friends. Their ancestors were wild wolves, which people began taming to help them hunt a few hundred years before villages were built.

True or False?

The first farmers used to milk cows.

FALSE. Animals were kept for their meat at first, and people started milking goats long before cows.

South American farmers kept guinea pigs.

TRUE. They also kept turkeys and llamas, and grew maize and sweet potatoes.

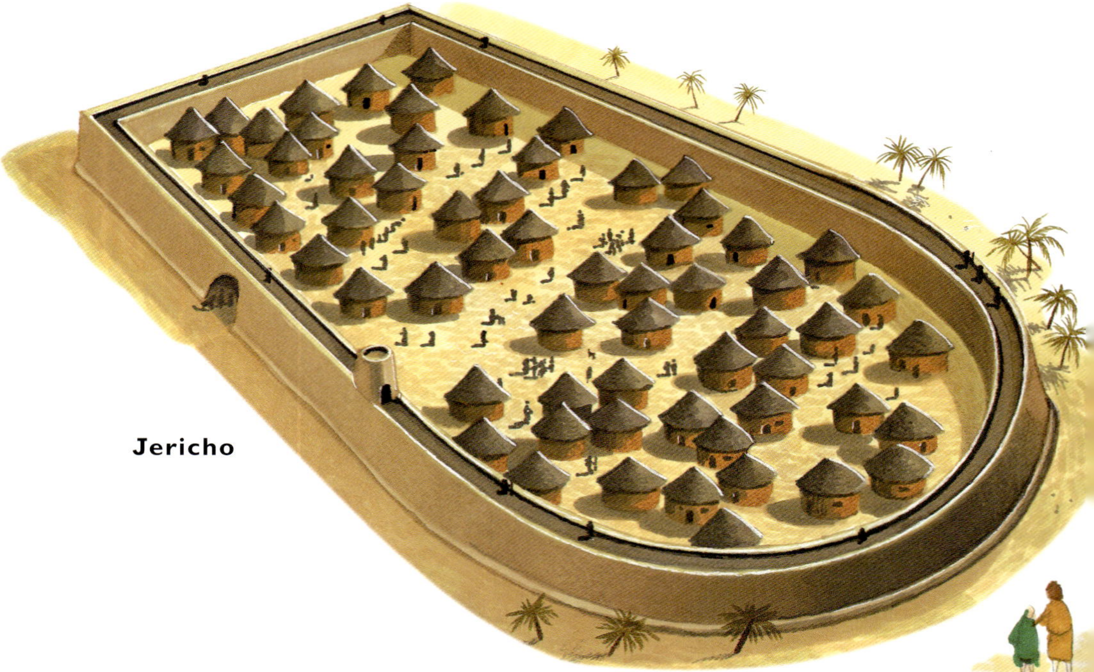

Jericho

When were the first towns built?

In some places, farmers were so successful that their villages grew into towns. The earliest we know about is Jericho in the Middle East. By about 9,000 years ago, it was surrounded by high stone walls and a deep ditch.

How big were they?

Jericho was home to at least 2,000 people, but around three times as many were living in Çatalhöyük in Turkey by 7,000 years ago. Unlike Jericho, with its bee-hive houses, Çatalhöyük was a warren of mud-brick boxes, with doors on the roof tops.

Çatalhöyük

True or False?

Part of Jericho is still standing.

TRUE. There's a circular stone tower with mud-plastered walls where you can still see the plasterers' fingerprints!

All townspeople were farmers.

FALSE. They did all sorts of work – for example, some of them were beadmakers or butchers.

When were the first cities built?

The first cities had grown up by 5,000 years ago, at the very end of the Stone Age. They were built by the people of Sumer, a land in the Middle East, and they were huge, with homes for tens of thousands of citizens.

What were they like?

At the heart of Sumerian cities like Ur were huge temples called ziggurats. All around were narrow winding streets packed with houses, shops and inns.

Ziggurat

What was special about the Sumerians?

The Sumerians were great inventors, and their most useful brainwave was coming up with the first proper writing. It's hard piecing together how Stone Age people lived because there were no written records. But from Sumerian times on, we start to get everything from histories to love poems and shopping lists.

Sumerian writing tablet

True or False?

The Sumerians wore trousers.

FALSE. Both men and women wore skirts and make-up.

The Sumerians played games.

TRUE. Experts have found a Sumerian board game, with a built-in drawer for all the pieces.

How were mummies made?

and other questions about early civilizations

Who built the pyramids?

The pyramids were built by the Ancient Egyptians as magnificent tombs for their kings, the pharaohs, and other very important people. The biggest is the Great Pyramid at Giza. It was 146.5 m high when it was built – taller than the Statue of Liberty is today.

Why did pharaohs need pyramids?

No one is certain, but we do know that the Egyptians believed the dead travelled to another world, the Afterlife. The sloping sides of the pyramids may have been like launch ramps, helping the pharaohs to shoot up to heaven.

Why were the Egyptians ancient?

We call them ancient because they lived so long ago – the Great Pyramid was finished in 2550 BC (before Christ was born – AD means after Christ's birth).

True or False?

The pyramids had secret entrances.

True. They were meant to stop robbers, but they didn't. There were over 80 pyramids – every one was robbed.

The Egyptians worshipped one god.

FALSE. They had thousands. Some paintings show gods with animal heads.

How did Egyptian men get to be mummies?

The Egyptians believed that their souls needed real bodies in the Afterlife, so they came up with ways of preserving the dead to stop them rotting away. These preserved bodies are what we call 'mummies'. Everybody who was anybody was mummified.

Mummification

How were mummies made?

The first stage in making a mummy was taking out the brain, lungs, heart, stomach, intestines and liver. Then the body was washed and left to dry out for 40 days in salty stuff called natron. Next up was a rub down in special oils. Finally, the body was carefully wrapped in linen bandages and put inside a nest of coffins.

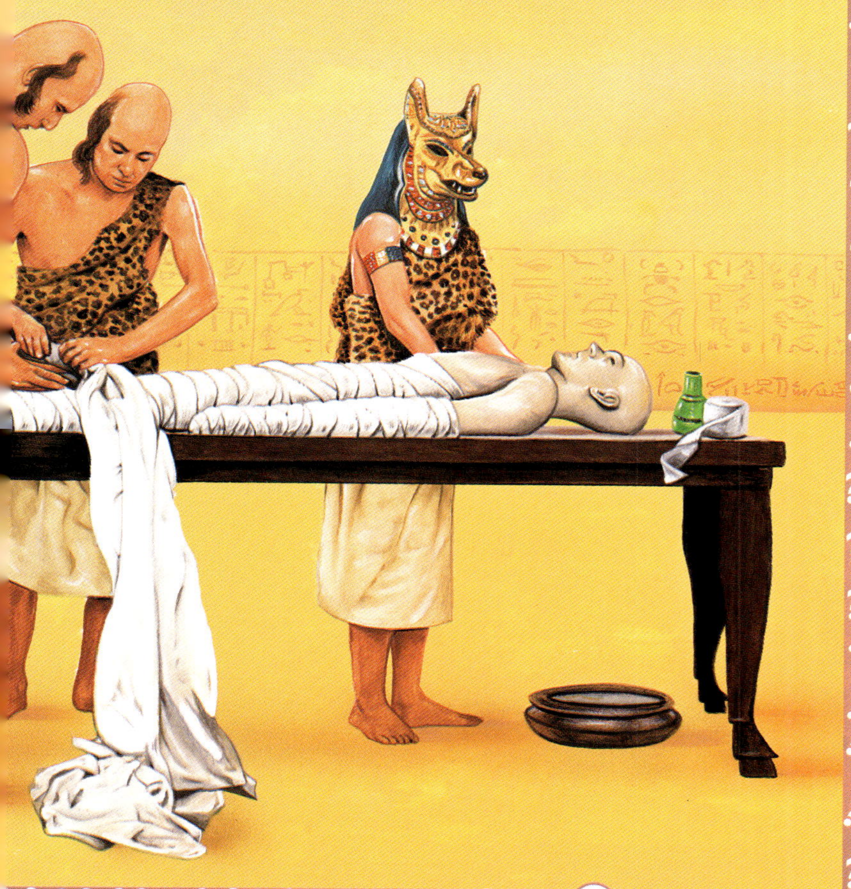

True or False?

Mummies were brainless.

TRUE. The brain was thrown away. The heart was put back in the body, and the other body parts were put in special stone jars.

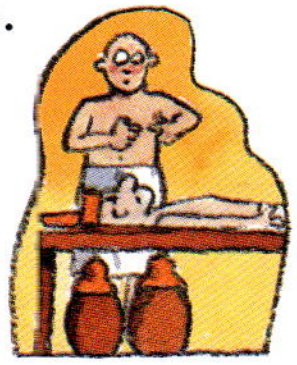

Only people were mummified.

FALSE. Sacred animals such as cobras, crocodiles, cats and even scarab beetles were also mummified.

Who was Tutankhamun?

Tutankhamun was only 17 when he died, but he's become Egypt's best-known pharaoh. He isn't famous for what he did when he was alive, but for the glittering treasures that were buried with him – including a magnificent gold face mask and a solid gold coffin!

Tutankhamun's mask

Did Egyptians throw good parties?

Pharaohs and rich people threw amazing parties, where they feasted on beef and antelope meat, and drank fine wines. There was entertainment too, from musicians, singers, dancers, acrobats and even magicians.

Ancient Egyptian party

Who hunted hippos?

Rich Egyptian men did – they loved taking a boat out on the River Nile to hunt hippos and crocodiles. Another favourite sport was taking a racing chariot out into the desert to hunt lions, gazelles and ostriches.

True or False?

All Egyptians ate beef.

FALSE. Poor people mainly ate bread, vegetables and dried fish. They drank beer.

Egyptians wore wigs.

TRUE. Pharaohs and rich people did, along with perfume, lipstick and eye make-up.

What were Egyptian homes like?

Egypt is a hot country where it hardly ever rains, so houses didn't need pointed roofs for rain to run off. Bricks were made from river mud mixed with straw and reed. Ordinary people's homes were quite small and simple, but rich people's were big with lots of rooms and a garden.

Egyptian house

Greek soldiers

Egyptian soldiers

Did children go to school?

Boys from rich families did and, like you, they had to learn to read and write. Egyptians wrote using picture symbols called hieroglyphs, and boys had to learn 700 of them off by heart.

Egyptian children

What happened to the Egyptians?

Although the Ancient Egyptians were once the most powerful nation in the world, by about 1000 BC their days of greatness were over. In 332 BC, Egypt was conquered by the Ancient Greeks and made part of their empire.

True or False?

Egyptian boys left school aged 18.

FALSE. They began school aged five and left at twelve years old.

Egyptian children played with toys.

TRUE. They had balls, marbles and spinning tops, as well as toy lions and horses made of wood.

Slaves had to water the Hanging Gardens of Babylon by hand, because they were created before hose pipes were invented!

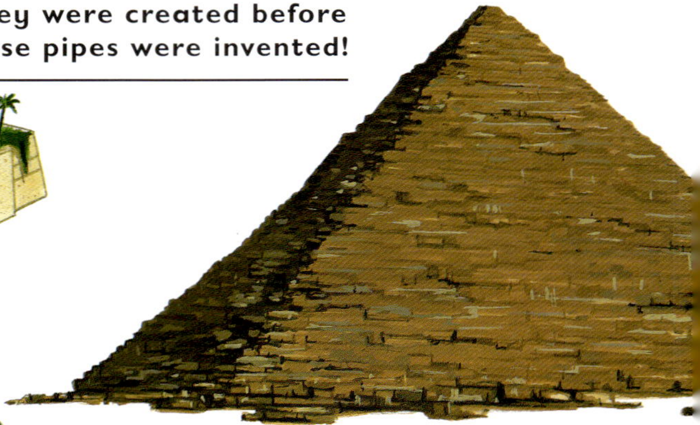

The Colossus of Rhodes was a huge bronze statue of the Greek sun god Helios. It was about as high as today's Statue of Liberty in New York.

What were the Seven Wonders?

The Seven Wonders were the top spots for tourists to visit in ancient times. They were built more than 2,200 years ago.

The pyramids at Giza are the oldest of the Wonders, and the only ones still standing today.

The gold and ivory Statue of Zeus at Olympia was over six times as high as a man.

The Lighthouse at Alexandria was more than 120 m high. The fire burning at its top could be seen by sailors far out at sea.

The Temple of Artemis at Ephesus was one of the largest temples of the ancient world.

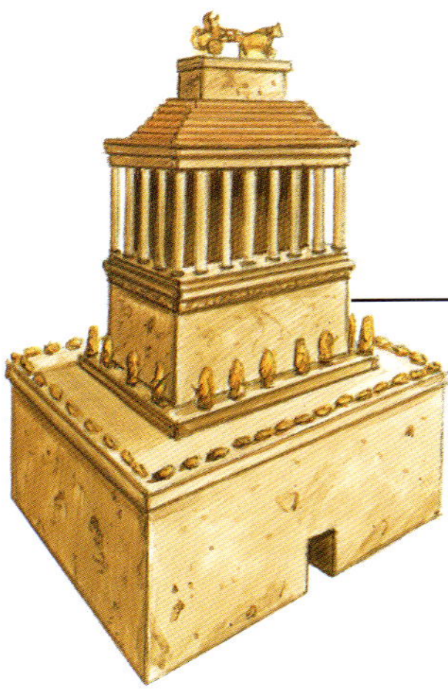

After the pyramids, the huge Mausoleum at Halicarnassus was the most famous tomb of ancient times.

True or False?

Most of the Wonders were designed by the Ancient Greeks.

TRUE. The Greeks made them all, except the Hanging Gardens and the pyramids.

The world's first zoo was in Alexandria.

TRUE. It had a leopard, a python, a giraffe and a polar bear.

Who were the Ancient Greeks?

By 700 BC, the Greek world was made up of lots of separate city-states, each formed from a city and the surrounding farmland. The biggest and most powerful city-states were Athens and Sparta.

Did the Greeks have armies?

They certainly did! The city-states were a quarrelsome lot and they often went to war. Only Sparta had a full-time army, though. The other city-states called freemen to arms when a war broke out.

Athenian soldiers

Did they have kings?

Most city-states were ruled by a king or a group of wealthy men at first. However, one of the Greeks' main claims to fame is the invention of people power. Democracy is a system of government in which people vote on how their country is run, and it was first put into practice in Athens in 508 BC.

Voting in Athens

Spartan soldiers

True or False?

Athenian women helped to run cities.

FALSE. Only freemen over the age of 17 did – women and slaves weren't allowed to vote.

The biggest city-states all had navies.

TRUE. Greek warships had a vicious metal spike in front – the idea was to ram and sink enemy ships.

What did Greeks eat for breakfast?

Porridge was a favourite at breakfast time, made with barley instead of oats and livened up with figs. Lunch was usually bread and goat's cheese, while dinner might be a tasty pigeon or chicken, with fresh fruit for pudding.

Who were the toughest Greeks?

The Spartans were as tough as nails. Instead of going to ordinary school, boys were taken away from their mothers and sent to army training camps at just 7 years old. To harden them up, they were kept cold and hungry and forced to go barefoot.

Spartan training camp

What did children learn at school?

Only Greek boys went to school – girls stayed at home and learnt how to run a household. School subjects included reading, writing, maths, music, athletics and public speaking. Schooling began when boys were 6 or 7, and lasted until they were 18-20 years old.

True or False?

Greek babies had potties.

TRUE. But Greek potties were made of pottery, not plastic!

Spartan girls were softies.

FALSE. Girls learnt to run, jump and wrestle, to toughen them up for having babies later on.

When were the Olympics first held?

The first Olympic Games were held in 776 BC, to honour Zeus, the chief of the Greek gods. They were held every four years, and thousands of athletes came from all over Greece to take part.

Were there swimming races?

No, the Greek Olympic events were running, boxing, wrestling, javelin and discus throwing, the long jump, horse racing and chariot racing.

Did athletes win medals?

No – winners were given small prizes at the Games, such as a crown of laurel leaves or a jar of olive oil. They were treated like superstars and showered with gifts and food when they got home, though.

Olympic champion

True or False?

Greek athletes never cheated.

FALSE. Some did. If they were caught, they had to pay for a statue to be put up.

Women were banned from the Olympics.

TRUE. They held their own Games in honour of the goddess Hera, Zeus's wife.

Why did the Greeks laugh at frogs?

One of the smash hit theatre plays in Ancient Greek times was Frogs by the playwright Aristophanes. The Greeks were the first people to build theatres and put on plays. The theatres were open air, and the actors were all men, wearing masks painted to show which character they were playing.

Philosophers

Greek theatre

Why were the Greeks wise?

The Greeks were great thinkers, who developed the art of philosophy – thinking about big questions such as the meaning of life. The most important Greek philosophers were Socrates, Plato and Aristotle.

Why was Alexander great?

Alexander the Great was a brilliant Greek general, who won a huge empire in the early 300s BC. This was the peak of Greek power. In 146 BC, the Romans took over Greece and made it part of their own empire.

Alexander the Great

True or False?

The Greeks were great storytellers.

TRUE. The most famous Greek works are the Iliad and the Odyssey – tales of war, heroes, gods and mythical beings.

Zeus and Hera were the only Greek gods.

FALSE. The Greeks believed in lots of gods and goddesses, including Aphrodite, goddess of love and beauty, and Ares, the god of war.

When was Stonehenge built?

Local tribespeople began building the great stone circles of Stonehenge in southern England in about 2100 BC. The circles were built in stages, and took a lot of hard work and hundreds of years to finish – the biggest stones weigh as much as ten elephants! Experts think the tribes used Stonehenge for religious ceremonies, perhaps for worshipping the Sun and the Moon.

Stonehenge

Great Wall of China

Who built the Great Wall of China?

Shih Huang-ti was a great Chinese ruler, who was the first to conquer other Chinese leaders and govern an empire. He ordered work to start on the Great Wall in about 220 BC. After he died, he was buried in a huge tomb, with a vast army of more than 6,000 life-sized pottery statues of his warriors and their horses.

True or False?

Stonehenge builders used horses and carts to shift the stones.

FALSE. The stones were brought to the site and put up using human muscle power.

The Great Wall is visible from space.

TRUE. It's the world's longest structure, at about 6,400 km long.

Which Roman babies were looked after by a wolf?

The Romans believed that Rome, their capital city in Italy, was established in 753 BC by a man called Romulus, the son of Mars, the god of war. Roman legends also told how Romulus and his twin brother Remus were stolen from their mother when they were babies, and thrown into the River Tiber. The twins were supposed to have been saved by a wolf, who fed and cared for them as if they were her own cubs.

Romulus, Remus and the wolf

Why was Julius Caesar stabbed to death?

Julius Caesar was a Roman politician who was murdered in 44 BC by fellow politicians – they feared he wanted to overthrow the democratic government and make himself king. The Romans did end up with a kind of king though, because in 27 BC Augustus Caesar became the first Roman emperor.

Julius Caesar

Murder of Julius Caesar

True or False?

Julius Caesar invaded Britain.

TRUE. He conquered France and invaded Britain twice.

Julius Caesar built Hadrian's Wall.

FALSE. The Emperor Hadrian started work on a huge stone wall across northern Britain in AD 122.

Tortoise

What did Roman soldiers do with tortoises?

The tortoise was a Roman attack formation. Soldiers made a tough tortoise-shell shape around themselves with their shields, as protection against enemy weapons.

Which weapons did Roman soldiers use?

Roman soldiers fought with spears and swords. Their armour included a helmet, a breastplate and, of course, a shield.

What did soldiers do when they weren't fighting?

It was a tough life in the Roman army. When they weren't fighting battles, soldiers were often hard at work building roads. Engineers used special measuring tools to work out the shortest and most direct route, which is why Roman roads are famous for being straight.

Roman road building

True or False?

The Romans invented concrete.

TRUE. The mixture was so tough that many Roman roads, bridges and buildings are still standing today.

Roman soldiers ate spaghetti.

FALSE. It hadn't been invented in Roman times. Soldiers ate bacon, cheese and biscuits.

Did the Romans watch clowns at the Circus?

No, the Circus Maximus was a famous stadium in Rome, where chariot races were held.

Thousands of people went every week to cheer their favourite team, rather like football matches today. Instead of club names, though, the teams had colours – blue, red, green and white.

Who gave the thumbs up to gladiators?

Another favourite day out was a visit to the amphitheatre to watch fighters called gladiators. Usually, pairs of gladiators fought until one of them was defeated and killed. But if the crowd was in a good mood, people would give the thumbs up sign to show they wanted the loser to live.

True or False?

Gladiators fought wild animals.

TRUE. They had to face panthers, leopards or even bears.

Only men fought as gladiators.

FALSE. Some women did. Like the men, they were criminals or war captives.

Why did Romans live in high-rises?

When space got tight in big cities like Rome, landlords built upwards – some blocks of flats were six storeys high. The flats were often badly built, and the ones in Rome were particularly famous for falling down.

Roman buildings

Roman wedding

When did girls get married?

Many Roman girls were married by their 12th birthday. Girls and boys from wealthy families went to school when they were 7, but girls left at 11 years old, and boys finished some time between their 16th and 18th birthdays.

What happened to the Romans?

At the height of their power, in the AD 100s, the Romans ruled much of Europe and the Middle East, as well as the north coast of Africa. The Empire then began to crumble. It was attacked by tribes from the north and the east, and in AD 476 a Germanic warrior called Odoacer declared himself king of Italy.

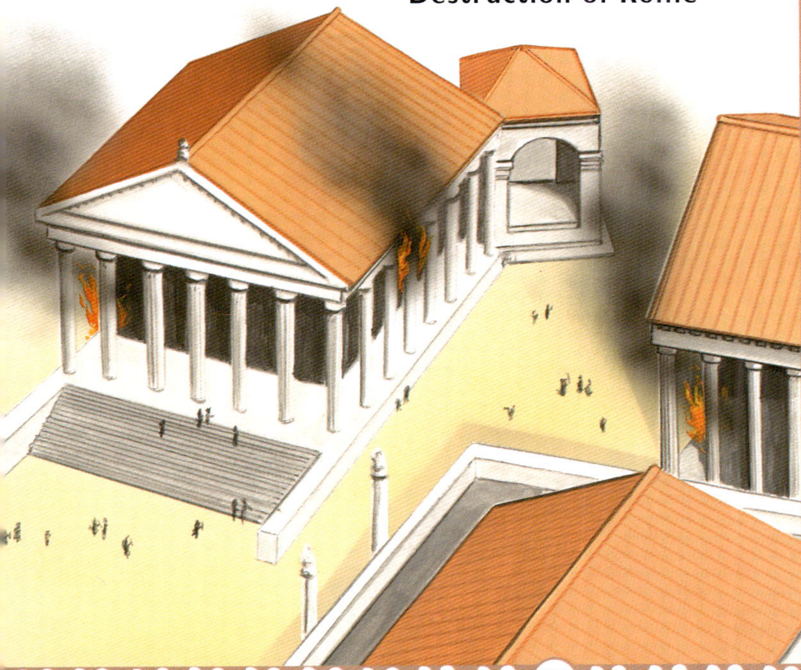

Destruction of Rome

True or False?

Rich people didn't live in blocks of flats.

TRUE. They built big luxurious villas, with underfloor heating, wall paintings and tiled floors.

The Romans ate stuffed dormice.

TRUE. Rich people had all sorts of exotic food, and they ate lying down on couches.

Index